INTELLIGENT BPM

THE NEXT WAVE

FOR CUSTOMER-CENTRIC BUSINESS APPLICATIONS

DR. SETRAG KHOSHAFIAN

FOREWORD BY ALAN TREFLER

© 2014 Pegasystems Inc.
Pegasystems Inc.
One Rogers St.
Cambridge, MA 02142
www.pega.com

ISBN 978-0-615-51512-0 Trademark notice: Product or corporate names may be trademarks or registered trademarks, and are used only for identification and explanation without intent to infringe.

TABLE OF CONTENTS

FOREWORD

Business and IT have been on a collision course for many years because technology traditionally has not done what the business has wanted. Because of this conundrum, organizations have had to change the way that they think about and approach technology in order to be successful with their projects. They have had to become more intelligent, and so has the way in which they manage their processes. This transition has aligned with the evolution of Business Process Management (BPM) to what Gartner has defined as intelligent Business Process Management (iBPM). iBPM has become THE new way of creating customer-centric software and agile business solutions. iBPM challenges and collapses the silos that separate business units. True iBPM empowers continuous improvement through continuously evolving automation. iBPM has spurred new levels of cooperation and collaboration between business and IT.

iBPM is transformational, putting customer outcomes at the heart of every process. Businesses empowered to change business software and achieve a rhythm of change and continuous improvement, have suddenly become reality. Business context and the business milieu now become actionable. iBPM automates not only mundane tasks and key business practices, but also dynamic knowledge work. This is a topic that I address in my forthcoming book *Customerpocalypse*. In essence, if today's businesses do not have the intelligence and ability to quickly adapt, they run the chance of being the next great business failures.

As iBPM automates work, it also learns and adapts. It is a platform that handles predetermined structured processes as well as dynamic unstructured collaboration across teams and geographies. It is an approach that intelligently guides human workers and makes them much more productive. It incorporates social networking and allows interaction through familiar Web browsers or mobile devices of choice, whenever and however desired, with client experiences seamlessly integrated across channels.

Simply, iBPM is about running the business. Better. And ALWAYS about responding to each customer situation with optimal business intelligence and the efficiency of dynamic automation.

Perhaps most importantly, iBPM helps organizations innovate. While the previous generations of BPM focused on process efficiencies, this new generation of BPM has empowered organizations to innovate and create new models to run their businesses and drive better outcomes.

Whether you are a novice in BPM or have been adopting BPM for improving your processes, you will find Setrag Khoshafian's insight invaluable in your BPM journey.

The book covers the fundamentals of iBPM, the role of iBPM in the enterprise ecosystem, legacy modernization and process improvement, and culminates by examining how Pega BPM is the modern way to build dynamic, customer-centric business applications.

At Pega, we have been intensely focused on providing both the ideal platform for business innovation, as well as solution frameworks to jump start solutions in many industries.

Today, organizations need to Build for Change® to achieve new levels of agility, enhance customer loyalty, generate new business and improve productivity. Pega is committed to driving innovation and the success of our clients in this critical mission. Please enjoy Setrag's exploration of iBPM practices and potential. We look forward to sharing this journey with you!

Alan Trefler
Founder & CEO
Pegasystems

Alan Trefler is the Founder and Chief Executive Officer of Pegasystems. He also serves as Chairman of the Pegasystems Board of Directors.

 Alan was named The American Business Award's "Software CEO of the Year" for 2009. He was also named "Public Company CEO of the Year" in 2011 by the Massachusetts Technology Leadership Council. Alan has frequently presented to international audiences, written for major publications, and consulted extensively in the use of advanced technologies and work automation. In 2011, Alan was a keynote presenter at the Baron Funds Conference. He has been profiled in national print and broadcast media including *CNBC*, *Fox Business News*, *Fortune Magazine*, *Inc. Magazine*, *Forbes*, *The Boston Globe*, *The New York Times*, *Bloomberg Television*, *Barron's*, *Reuters*, and *Investor's Business Daily*. Alan has also been named the inventor of five issued US patents and several US and international patent applications for Pegasystems' distinctive Inherited Rule-Based Architecture, which provides the framework for Pegasystems' rules-based Business Process Management (BPM) solutions.

Alan's interest in computers originates from collegiate involvement in tournament chess, where he achieved a Master rating and was co-champion of the 1975 World Open Chess Championship. His passion and support for chess and the game's community and current champions continues to this day. Alan holds a degree with distinction in Economics and Computer Science from Dartmouth College.

ABOUT THE AUTHOR

Dr. Setrag Khoshafian is one of the industry's pioneers and recognized experts in iBPM. He has been a senior executive in the software industry for the past 25 years, where he has invented, architected, and led the production of several enterprise software products and solutions.

 Currently, he is Pegasystems' Chief Evangelist and strategic iBPM technology thought leader involved in numerous technology, marketing, alliance, and customer initiatives.

His interests and expertise span all aspects of iBPM in the enterprise, including Predictive and Adaptive iBPM, Internet and Process of Everything, Dynamic Case Management, Social iBPM, iBPM for SOA, iBPM for Legacy Modernization and Business Transformation, Real-Time Lean Six Sigma, iBPM Methodologies, Centers of Excellence , and Organizational Impact of iBPM.

Previously he was the Senior VP of Technology at Savvion, a senior architect at Ashton-Tate, and OODBMS researcher at MCC. Dr. Khoshafian has authored ten books and numerous reviewed articles on iBPM and advanced database management systems.

He is a frequent speaker and presenter at international workshops and conferences. This book on iBPM is the second edition of his previous book titled: *BPM: The Next Wave for Business Applications*. He is also the author of the seminal work: *Service-Oriented Enterprises*[1] that focused on the cultural service dimension as well as the emerging architecture of service orientation. It showed how by aligning business and IT, business process management (BPM) has become the core layer of SOEs.

Dr. Khoshafian holds a PhD in Computer Science from the University of Wisconsin-Madison. He also holds an MSc in Mathematics.

Blog: http://www.pega.com/community/pega-blog/33684 iBPM
Professor: http://www.pega.com/products/bpm/bpm-professor

---

[1] Available at http://www.pega.com/featured/soe

ACKNOWLEDGEMENTS

This book was made possible through the support, encouragement, and contributions of many Pegasystems' resources. First and foremost, I would like to thank Alan Trefler for his vision, leadership, and the foreword for this book. It is a privilege to contribute to Pega's market leadership in iBPM, and Alan made that possible. I also would like to thank Leon Trefler, Pega's Senior Vice President of Sales, for his support and encouragement. The original idea for this book came from Leon. The content and the flow of the book follow the iBPM Professor series, available on **www.pega.com**, which we started through the efforts of Eric Deitert.

Lauren St. Amand, Director Field Marketing, was the overall project manager. Lauren did a terrific job managing and coordinating the production effort on a tight budget and schedule. Notable mention should be made of the book's project team, especially Brendan McKenna—who did a great job editing this book—and Claire Larrabee for copy editing and proof reading. I would like to thank Brian Callahan, Director of Public Relations, for many contributions including edits to the foreword, provisioning the quotes and overall PR for the book. Also would like to thank Frank Tutalo and Andy Dear for the PR and social networking promotion of the book.

I would like to thank especially Katie Rezza as well as David Marrano and Sara Fix for the book's art work and illustrations. As you can see, they did a terrific job. I also would like to especially thank Stephen Zisk, Senior Manager Product Marketing, for his many contributions and edits.

Throughout the past few years, I have had the privilege of engaging in constructive thought leadership exchanges with many of my colleagues at Pega. It will be difficult to list them all. I would like to thank Max Mayer, Pega's Senior Vice President of Corporate Development, and Louis Blatt, Pega's Senior Vice President of Business Unit Management, for their perceptive leadership on Pega messages and positions reflecting various industry trends. I also especially appreciate the efforts of Product Management, under the leadership of Kerim Akgonul and Product Development, and Mike Pyle. Through their efforts they have made Pega *the* leader in iBPM and Dynamic Case Management.

Colleagues who provided helpful support and insight for this book from the marketing leadership team include especially Dave Donelan, Vice President Field and Partner Marketing; Douglas Kim, Managing Director Product Marketing; Steve Kraus, Senior Director of Product Marketing; Russell Keziere, who oversees Pega Corporate Marketing; and especially Bridget LaBrode, Executive Assistant, for her outstanding communication and helpfulness. Other notable mentions include Stephen Bixby, Senior Director of Product Management, John Petronio, Director of Product Marketing, and Ken Schwarz, Director of BPM and Case Management Product Marketing.

I am also grateful to the thought leadership interactions that I have had with a number of colleagues: Rob Walker, Vice President Decision Management Analytics, Peter van der Putten, Director Decision Solutions, and Keijzer Maarten, Senior Director Product Management Decision Analytics on Predictive and Adaptive Analytics as well as Adaptive Enterprises; Don Schuerman, Senior Director Solutions Architecture, on Process of Everything; and Erik Moti, Manager Solutions Consulting, and Sushil Kumar, Senior Director COE Architecture, on Legacy Modernization. I also appreciated exchanges and discussions with Paul Roeck, Senior Director of BPM Adoption Services, and his team on iBPM COE and Methodology. Other notables include John Barone, John Everhard, and Bruce Williams.

Last, but definitely not least, I would like to thank my wife Silva, who had to put up with yet another book project.

Why iBPM and not iBPM Suite or System?

This book is about *intelligent* Business Process Management. Technology is critical, and Gartner (www.Gartner.com) calls the leading application infrastructures that support BPM projects and programs *Business Process Management Suites* [http://www.gartner.com/it-glossary/bpms-business-process-management-suite/]. It has also been called BPM *systems*.

However, BPM is much more than technology. BPM is at its core a transformational management discipline that helps organizations achieve their strategic goals. Automation is a key component of BPM solutions. As a discipline, BPM drives the operations of enterprises. It includes several iterative phases from design to execution to monitoring and continuous improvement. It plays a key role in process improvement and enterprise architectures.

The *intelligent* adjective represents an important evolution and milestone in BPM. Gartner introduced the term and acronym iBPM Suites (http://www.gartner.com/DisplayDocument?doc_cd=224913&ref=g_sitelink).

iBPMS encapsulates a number of core capabilities, including:

* Process Execution and State Management Engine
* Model-Driven Composition Environment
* Document and Content Interaction
* User and Group Interaction
* Basic Connectivity
* Business Activity Monitoring (BAM) and Business Event Support
* Simulation and Optimization
* Business Rules Management (BRM)
* Management and Administration
* Process Component Registry/Repository

iBPM suites are ideal for *intelligent* business operations. Key among intelligent business operations are iBPM-enabled customer relationship management operations.

So to represent the holistic end-to-end discipline of realizing strategic objectives, as well as the increased ubiquity of the BPM suite or platform, we have used intelligent BPM—iBPM—throughout this book, with the full understanding that the iBPM Suite with all its components and capabilities are not only covered extensively in the book, but constitute the core of the iBPM transformational discipline.

CHAPTER 1

What is iBPM?

This book is about the next wave for customer-centric business applications through intelligent Business Process Management (iBPM). What is iBPM? iBPM is a transformational discipline that helps organizations achieve their strategic goals. iBPM spans several iterative phases, from design to execution to monitoring and continuous improvement. It plays a key role in process improvement and enterprise architectures. Perhaps most importantly, iBPM helps organizations achieve robust customer centricity by automating their policies and procedures. The evolution of iBPM was a long journey. Intelligent Business Process Management has evolved from advances in process improvement, business transformation, work automation, business rules, analytics, enterprise architecture, the Internet, and social collaboration.

The iBPM disciplines and technologies are enabling the emergence of the "adaptive enterprise." Through iBPM, an adaptive enterprise continuously aligns its business objectives to operationalized policies and procedures with complete transparency, visibility, and control. More importantly, an adaptive enterprise is agile and proactive in responding to change. After all, the only constant in business is change!

Policies and Procedures

A business is a collection of policies and procedures. Now, where are these policies and procedures derived from?

 Policy & Procedure Manuals: Whether you're dealing with operations in the front-, mid- or back-office, there are policy and procedure manuals. Without iBPM, workers need to be trained to follow the documented descriptions of policies and procedures, resulting in manual, expensive, and error-prone processing.

 People's (Knowledge Workers') Heads: Often, there are designated experts, or knowledge workers, who have the policies and procedures—the business rules—in their heads. The challenge is to harvest these policies and procedures. With iBPM, knowledge workers can participate in the automated processes as well as collaborative, dynamic cases.

Legacy Code: Another source of policies and procedures is legacy code that contains business logic. The embedded policies are often ossified in legacy code with little or no business visibility. They are difficult to change or extend. The challenge is to leverage legacy systems, while allowing the organization to modernize and be agile. It is like changing the oil in a car while the engine is still running. iBPM can modernize and transform incumbent legacies.

 Data: Sometimes the behavior of customers is hidden in operational databases, historic data warehouses, and increasingly in "big data" that needs to be mined and operationalized. Through data mining techniques, predictive customer behavior models can be discovered from data. The challenge then becomes the execution or operationalization of the discovered models. iBPM provides the context for executing predictive decisions.

 Modeling: In other situations, enterprises embark upon modeling initiatives to capture "as-is" models to see how they can improve them and create "to-be" models. Often, such modeling initiatives result in voluminous documentation and modeling artifacts with little business impact or business value.

 Intelligent Business Process Management is about business process *automation*: not only capturing the policies and procedures in the iBPM system as models, but automating these models, operationalizing them, and allowing the business to continuously monitor and improve.

Execution Gaps

Every decade or so, a new technology trend arrives with the promise of finally resolving the conundrum of adaptive enterprise connectivity and efficiency. There are many solutions and technologies that are attempting to gain mindshare for business solutions. Some of these include enabling technologies such as social networking and the cloud. However, iBPM provides the most agile, unified, aggregated and viable platform to build business solutions. An iBPM solution specifically addresses the "execution gaps" between business objectives and the execution of business activities.

Traditionally, IT departments attempt to keep up with business execution through information systems. This approach has inherent limitations and has not been able to keep up with business demands. Why the gap? Well, partly because IT and business have different priorities. Business is, first and foremost, focused on revenue. Business objectives are also tightly associated with market share and the branding of products and services. Other high-level objectives include improvements in productivity, compliance, cost reduction, as well as innovation by a well-oiled adaptive enterprise with satisfied customers and stakeholders. IT, on the other hand, focuses on providing the necessary support and execution of systems that can help achieve the business objectives, using intensely technical platforms, tools, and primitives. There are legacy and proprietary systems that are difficult to extend. These traditional IT issues—from maintenance to increased backlogs and requirements for new applications—are augmented with new challenges, especially globalization and compliance.

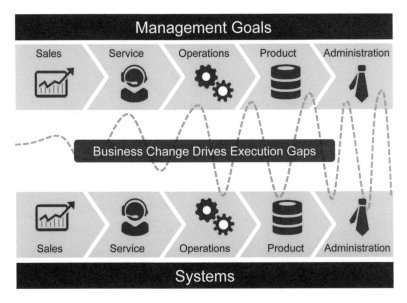

Today, organizations are increasingly facing pressures to change and respond to multiple types of challenges. These can come from internal stakeholders, customers, the government, and shareholders alike. As organizations migrate to emerging enterprise solutions, the frequency and magnitude of change is increasing. Market pressures, the need to integrate diverse departments, and global competition are driving management to constantly evolve the 'rules' of the business, resulting in a massive increase of changes in business policies and procedures. Since iBPM solutions automate policies and procedures, they stand the best chance of reducing or even eliminating the execution gaps, while allowing the business to keep up with change. The next sections delve into each of the letters of the acronym: "B," "P," and "M" as well as the "i" or the *intelligence* of iBPM.

Business: The "B" in iBPM

Let's talk about iBPM, starting with the **business**. iBPM is not just about technology: It is the discipline of building solutions with a business focus. How?

- **Business Objectives:** Businesses have objectives. These are often measurable objectives such as Key Performance Indicators (KPIs) to grow revenue, cut costs, or increase customer satisfaction. Through iBPM, the business can drill down from their high-level KPIs to automated business processes, gaining complete visibility and control.

- **Business Requirements:** Businesses have requirements that need to be operationalized and automated. Through iBPM, businesses can have a common *lingua franca* with IT and directly realize their requirements within the iBPM tool.
- **Context for Business Assets:** Businesses need to treat customers uniquely, based on a particular set of criteria. iBPM can provide the context and specific solutions for their specific customers or lines of business. Through iBPM, enterprises can easily reuse and specialize their business assets.
- **Innovation and Change:** Businesses need to innovate in order to compete. They also need to be able to introduce change, and do it very quickly to respond to market demands. Here again, iBPM is the ideal platform for innovation in products and services. More importantly, iBPM allows organization to be adaptive and responsive to changes in business objectives, customer behavior, and market conditions.

So, iBPM solutions are about business process *automation*. iBPM enables the business to directly capture their objectives and to manage change. This change can happen through easy-to-use process modeling constructs such as business rule, process, and case models. With iBPM, the business has the power to directly introduce changes in order to meet their objectives.

Process: The "P" in iBPM

BPM suites focus on the **process** by automating the work. iBPM suites make it easy to **receive** work that needs processing. Work can be received across various channels including a Web browser, phone, mail, mobile, web services, and others. iBPM then **routes** the work to systems or people based on skill, workload, priorities, or service levels. iBPM organizes related work into dynamic cases which can then be prioritized and managed. iBPM also keeps track of all the activities and tasks that execute within the various business process solutions. This is known as real-time business activity **reporting**. It is extremely important for the business to coordinate and control its objectives, and have complete visibility as to what is happening throughout its operations. The business can drill down from these KPIs or reports and make changes, such as reassigning tasks if certain processes are not on schedule.

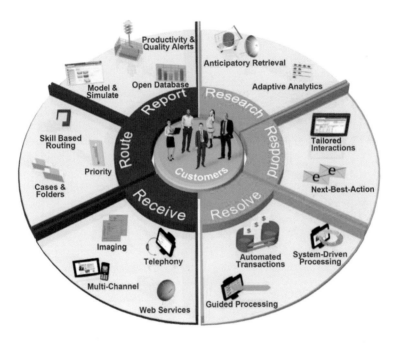

The iBPM engine also does **research**. This means that it dynamically gets data as needed and when needed by going to the best sources. These are often legacy systems of record or back-end systems. iBPM solutions use predictive and adaptive analytics to ensure that interactions are on target. It recommends the Next-Best-Action[2] in customer interactions. It responds contextually depending upon the customer, the product, and the location, and can generate automated correspondence. iBPM enables business solution customers, partners, or other

---

[2] "Next-Best-Action" means real-time decisioning is applied using predictive models, adaptive models as well as business rules to identify optimal ("best") actions in iBPM solutions.

parties to collaborate. This brings us to *resolving* the work, which means driving it through the processes and the associated business rules towards completion. iBPM suites automate work as much as possible, and when human participants or operators are involved, the iBPM suite assists them through guided interactions.

Management: The "M" in iBPM

How about **management** in iBPM? There are at least three complimentary aspects of management:

- Managing Business Performance: With the help of enterprise process automation, the business is able to do real-time activity monitoring. iBPM keeps track of the execution of each automated process and maintains an audit trail of the assigned tasks, the performance of operators or workers, and the performance of individual processes or iBPM solutions. Businesses can take any of their KPIs and drill down to affect change. For instance, they can bulk re-assign the tasks of operators who are not able to keep up with their service levels.

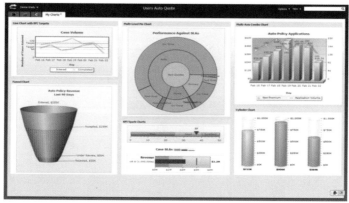

- Managing Change: With iBPM, the organization can easily introduce business policy or procedural changes while reusing assets across the organization. Often, the business can be empowered to make changes directly. These assets include process flows, decision rules, case types, constraints, expressions, user interfaces (UI), and integration. They can be organized along a number of dimensions such as product type, customer, or location. At run-time, the iBPM provides contextual or situational execution of the asset at the moment when it is needed. Through iBPM, the business can be empowered to introduce incremental changes to business rules and processes.

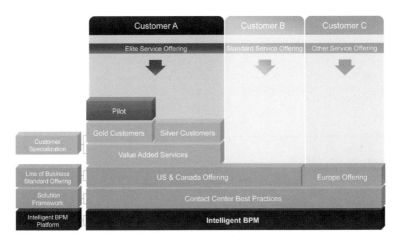

- Managing Business Solutions with Agility and Continuous Improvement: Through iBPM, businesses can prioritize as "slivers" the various initiatives or projects they have for improvement or optimization. Each sliver represents a low-hanging fruit that can demonstrate a quick improvement or win with demonstrable business value. The business can automate business solutions through iterative iBPM methodologies. The iBPM system can construct, wizard, and provide accelerated assistance throughout the iterations and continuous improvement lifecycle of the solution. The business, in collaboration with IT, can deploy solutions very quickly, and then observe the behavior and performance of the automated processes. It can then introduce incremental changes through continuous improvement cycles.

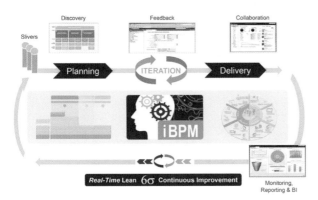

The "i" in iBPM

What about the *intelligent* in iBPM? There are many reasons for the "i" in iBPM:

- Dynamic Case Management: iBPM supports both planned, structured flows and dynamic cases involving knowledge workers. Cases reflect how we like to work—socially, collaboratively, responsively—and can include many participants to handle exceptions. Dynamic cases involve the organization of tasks in a case hierarchy. Cases can respond to or generate business events.

- Social iBPM: iBPM solutions leverage social tools, providers, and metaphors in all phases of iBPM solution lifecycles. Most importantly, iBPM provides the context for social networking and collaboration.
- Mobile iBPM: iBPM allows organizations to seamlessly initiate and complete automated case work from end-to-end via mobile devices. The instant accessibility of case status, case work, and case collaboration via mobile empowers a whole new category of mobile workers.
- Cloud iBPM: With the cloud, you can have enterprise applications that are built securely using the iBPM platform on the cloud: iBPM for Platform as a Service (PaaS). Once the iBPM solution is built and deployed, it can also execute or run on the cloud: iBPM Software as a Service (SaaS).
- Business Rules in iBPM: Business rules implement business decisioning logic and business policies, and these rules drive iBPM solutions. There are many categories and types of business rules such as decision trees, decision tables, constraints, and expressions. The focus on business rules is on externalizing the business logic—as close to the business as possible—without worrying about execution time, execution method, or execution order. Business rules are declarative. Predictive modeling techniques can be used to detect business patterns and then invoke or operationalize the discovered rules in the context of iBPM solutions.
- Analytics and Adaptive iBPM for Real-Time Decisioning: One of the most important trends in the industry is the emergence of data science and especially big data analytics. Predictive analytics are delivering tangible benefits to organizations by unlocking the insights hidden in vast amounts of digital information. iBPM, through both predictive and adaptive (self-learning) analytics, enables the insight that is discovered to become actionable. The "actions" are the decisions that the participants (e.g. customer service representatives (CSR) or marketing operators) make in robust intelligent BPM interactions. The sources and types of data that can be mined for actionable models in iBPM are heterogeneous and span social networks, transactional data, data warehouses and social network stores. iBPM solutions leverage predictive and adaptive models to provide the Next-Best-Action in various dynamic case interactions.

Therefore iBPM solutions are dynamic, social, mobile, rules-driven, and adaptive. These solutions can continuously analyze, learn and adapt from external events or the behavior of constituents and participants. iBPM provides the platform, solutions, best practices, methodologies and governance for adaptive enterprises.

The Evolution of iBPM

There are five trends that have evolved and culminated as iBPM including: *Process Improvement, Process Automation, Process Intelligence, Process Architecture*, and *Process Participants.*

- Process Improvement: The evolution of improvement in process efficiency and productivity within organizations goes back to Taylorism, or Scientific Management. In the 1990s, business process re-engineering took a top-down approach for process improvement and reorganization. Due to the radical amount of change attempted, most re-engineering initiatives did not succeed. Process improvement methodologies, such as Lean and Six Sigma, attempt to eliminate waste in work processing, while increasing the efficiency as well as the effectiveness and quality of products or services. Theory of Constraints and Net Promoter Scores (NPS)[3] provide robust and complementary improvement frameworks. The key point is that, whether improving NPS or critical-to-quality measurements for a Lean Six Sigma project, iBPM allows organizations to keep these measurements as well as control the customer experience and operational efficiency in real time.

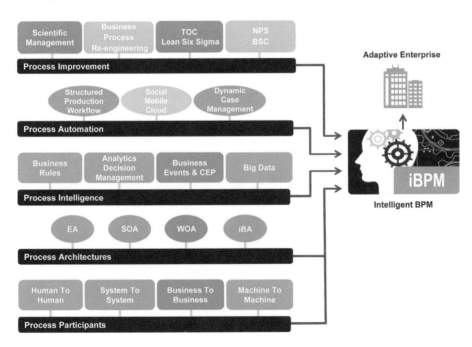

---

[3] Net Promoter Score, Net Promoter and NPS are registered trademarks of Bain & Company, Satmetrix Systems and Fred Reichheld.

- **Process Automation:** Automation has also evolved from structured production workflows into collaborative, unstructured, and dynamic cases. Production, or structured, workflow BPM focuses on predetermined, clerical or transactional work. Social and mobile technologies are expanding the scope of automation empowering connectivity as well as engagement of different categories of workers—especially knowledge workers and knowledge-assisted workers. Cases are holistic, involving tasks organized in a case hierarchy and aggregating information and content from many sources. They can handle unstructured and collaborative work with social and mobile capabilities, as well as structured production workflow. Cases are also dynamic, adding or changing any of their elements often during the course of work, driving towards a concrete business objective or goal. Dynamic cases respond to and generate events and can adapt when requirements, behaviors, circumstances, or events change.
- **Process Intelligence:** The intelligence in processes emanates from a number of core capabilities in an iBPM system. These include a rich collection of business rule types, predictive analytics, adaptive (learning) decisioning, event rules, and recommendations from big data.[4] Business rules—such as constraints, decision trees/tables, expressions, etc.—are an integral part of business process solutions. A business is a collection of policies (often implemented as business rules) and procedures (often implemented as process flows or cases.) Often this process intelligence is harvested from knowledge workers. Other sources include policy manuals and legacy code. Increasingly, the intelligence is mined and harvested from data. The sources and types of data vary and can include process or case data, transactional data, data from data warehouses, data from social networks, and of course the increasingly popular big data. Predictive and adaptive analytics mine these data sources to create actionable predictive models.
- **Process Architecture:** An enterprise architecture (EA) is the blueprint of the enterprise, capturing business, application, information, and infrastructure models and their relationships. An EA attempts to modernize legacy systems and govern change through complex organizations. Service-oriented architectures (SOA) and Web-oriented architectures (WOA) are important patterns that provide the ability to loosely couple applications, trading partners, and organizations via standards. Increasingly, business applications are becoming iBPM application, or at least are modernized through an iBPM agility layer. With the emergence of the cloud, infrastructure is being outsourced as a service. The most important trend is to combine data, process, and intent to optimize the customer experience via a revamped business architecture based on iBPM.
- **Process Participants:** The last, but perhaps most important trend is the evolution of the process participants. BPM has its roots in human participant-focused workflow systems. The coordination in this category is human-to-human. While some traditional BPM technologies and methods are still purely workflow-focused, iBPM is much more than that. Other significant categories of software

---

4 Wikipedia. "Big Data." Last Modified July 29, 2013. http://en.wikipedia.org/wiki/Big_data

that have influenced the evolution of iBPM include Enterprise Application Integration (EAI) and business-to-business (B2B) integration, which enables system-to-system and human-to-system iBPM. With Internet of Everything[5] (IoE) we now have a new category of machine-to-machine (M2M) integration. iBPM coordinates all these participants (humans, systems, and machines/devices) in complex, dynamic processes and cases to achieve business objectives.

- Process of Everything[6]: The Internet of Everything (IoE) is the most important technology trend. It will involve billions of devices or "Things" connected over the Internet—generating data, sensing, firing and consuming events, and being controlled remotely. From cities, to innovative businesses, to intelligent buildings, to farmlands and residences, the IoE is changing entire ecosystems. Every day new intelligent Things are joining the IoE. The trend is starting to generate considerable amounts of data. As more and more intelligent Things join this ecosystem, opportunities for innovation increase. Intelligent Things augment humans with increased automation and efficiencies, which ultimately improve life. iBPM provides the context as well as the container for intelligent Things to collaborate to achieve objectives. Key iBPM capabilities such as business rules, event correlation, analytics, and especially dynamic case management are ideal for this spectrum of participants collaborating for continuous improvement and the optimization of objectives. In the next couple of decades, semi– or even fully automated human robots and avatars

---

5 Cisco (2013). "Internet of Everything."http://www.cisco.com/web/about/ac79/innov/IoE.html
6 For more details see "Process of Everything" in iBPMS: Intelligent BPM Systems, 2013, edited by Layna Fischer. Lighthouse Point, Florida: Future Strategies, Inc., Book Division.

will become increasingly pervasive. iBPM is about automation involving different categories of participants, including intelligent Things in dynamic cases, with Things collaborating with humans and systems to complete tasks and drive business outcomes. Additionally, intelligent Things or software agents[7] can also assist human workers in iBPM solutions. In fact, automated processing and the processing of dynamic cases—all through the iBPM platform—provide the best milieu to leverage and demonstrate the potential of this new generation of intelligent workers. As this trend matures, humans will increasingly be focusing on innovation and cognitive work, delegating the routine and even the knowledge assistant work to automated Things. So, a new era in process automation is on the Internet horizon. This is the Process of Everything (PoE).

All these trends are culminating in iBPM, which has become the platform that enables an organization to realize the promise of the **adaptive enterprise**. With iBPM, stakeholders will have complete visibility and control of their objectives, which are often expressed in their KPIs or enterprise performance measures. They can see and understand what is going on with their support, mission-critical, or management processes. More importantly, they can be proactive and make changes to improve. iBPM enables business stakeholders to be in the driver's seat—monitoring, improving, innovating through new solutions, automating process work, and building efficiencies throughout. In other words, iBPM is about running the business with agility, efficiency, and customer-centric effectiveness!

---

[7] See "Agent Technology: An Overview" by James Odell, http://www.jamesodell.com/Agent_Technology-An_Overview.pdf

CHAPTER 2

Who Benefits from iBPM?

In Chapter 1, we answered the question: What is intelligent BPM? In this chapter we will discuss who benefits from iBPM. The short answer is everyone. Everyone includes the customer, the business, operations, and IT. This end-to-end and holistic benefit of iBPM is extremely important. iBPM is not just for the business, though the business reaps tremendous benefits from iBPM solutions. By the same token it is not just for IT, though IT will be able to modernize its architecture, deliver high quality solutions on time and gain incredible productivity. Given the very nature of business transformation, iBPM is the *only* approach to cover improvement for *all* stakeholders. Customers (or trading partners in B2B scenarios) benefit with consistent and high quality services that improve and transform the customer experience. The business gains the ability to respond to different types of market demands. Operators or workers also benefit, whether they are a knowledge worker, a clerical worker, or a knowledge-assisted worker, such as a customer service representative. These workers will be empowered with efficiencies that help them to focus on their tasks.

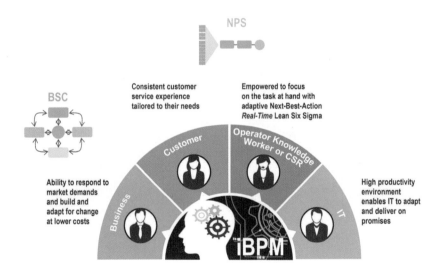

Benefits for Customers: Transforming the Customer Experience

Every business claims to be customer-centric. However, few organizations can achieve a true customer experience transformation. iBPM allows quantitative and qualitative customer expectations to be directly linked to internal processes, from the front-office to the back-office. Today, the power has shifted from product-centric companies to vocal customers, empowered especially through social media channels[8]. These empowered customers interact with peers and multiple channels online and easily switch providers if their needs are not met. Net Promoter Scores[9] and enterprise performance scorecards are pervasively compelling organizations to be ever-more driven by specific measures of their performance, identifying constraints, adapting, and acting.

There are three essential components of customer relationship management (CRM): marketing automation, sales force automation, and customer service and support (see Chapter 14). With iBPM-enabled CRM, there is complete visibility, transparency, and agility of processes supporting automation in CRM. Changes or customization to any aspect of CRM processes can easily be achieved, often by the business. Customer experience optimizations can be readily achieved in enterprises that are aggregated and connected via dynamic cases that involve all the processes in an organization that can affect the promoter scores.

There is also a cultural shift. Different customers prefer to be treated differently, depending on *their* context or situation. In order to meet the varying needs of today's complex customers, companies need to offer more than an exceptional product or service; they must provide an exceptional customer experience. Customer experience has been commonly defined as the sum of all experiences a customer has with a supplier of goods or services over the duration of the relationship with that supplier. A great customer experience is also a positive emotional connection that a customer has with a company, often resulting in a long-term relationship. This is developed by a company's ability to answer client concerns at the right time, at the right place, and across the appropriate channels. Companies have a significant opportunity to differentiate themselves by providing great customer experiences and maximizing customer lifetime value. This experience is not just about service, with timely and high quality responses. It is also about innovation, agility in making changes based on customer feedback, empowering the customer and truly making them a partner. Delivering this type of experience results in complete visibility and control for the organization, but more importantly, it allows customer service representatives to better service the customers.

iBPM supports the customer experience transformation through a number of essential capabilities:

- **Real-Time Sentiment Analysis and Processing of Social Media Postings or Exchanges with Real-Time Improvement:** Traditional customer service solutions expect the customer to make inbound contacts directly to the enterprise. With

---

[8] For a deep dive on the emerging "Generation C" and "Generation D" customers see Alan Trefler's book *Customerpocalypse* (2013).
[9] Net Promoter Score, Net Promoter and NPS are registered trademarks of Bain & Company, Satmetrix Systems and Fred Reichheld.

social media, it is the responsibility of the enterprise to continuously monitor customer communications, and based on those communications adapt the customer experience to ensure it is optimal. Social media has become a powerful channel for customers to provide their commentary on products and services. Customers increasingly leverage social media tools such as forums, blogs, social networking sites, podcasts, RSS feeds, wikis, and others to express opinions about products and services, exchange commentary, and interact. Organizations are starting to notice the impact of this social-media driven voice of the customer on their bottom line. Social media posting can go viral in an instant, sometimes with devastating results, as disgruntled customers express their impressions publicly on social networks. Through iBPM, organizations can leverage data mining and then handle the monitored and analyzed voice of the customer using automated processes and cases.

- **Holistic, Ad-hoc and Dynamic Cases to Readily Handle Customer Needs:** In addition to supporting predetermined and structured processes, organizations need to be able to dynamically add or adjust tasks that are often introduced through circumstances or events that result from the real-time processing of social media postings or inbound customer interactions. Enterprises proactively need to monitor (either through human or automated tools) and introduce ad-hoc tasks in customer case processes. When improving the customer experience, enterprises need to remove potential gaps that exist between inbound customer interactions and back-office systems that are required to resolve customer requests, disputes, or feedback. Social media interactions, exchanges, and feedback need to be an integral part of an umbrella case that involves both internal (to the organization) and external (especially social media) sources. Furthermore, these cases need to be able to handle *dynamic, ad-hoc and collaborative tasks*, as well as planned tasks.
- **Consistent Experience across Channels:** In addition to the silos between front- and back-office processes, there are also silos between channels in many organizations. The experience of the customer ends up depending on the channel! Furthermore, the context of the interaction from one channel is lost when it is transferred to another. With iBPM, the organization is able to provide consistent, high quality and targeted experiences across multiple channels including Web-based self-service sites,

contact centers, mobile devices and social network sites. Dynamic case management solutions are built once in iBPM and leveraged across all channels, consistently.

- Customer-centric, Tailored Experience for each Situation to Treat Different Customers Differently: Enterprises are increasingly differentiating themselves through personalized and situational or contextual treatment of customers, such as who the customer is, the customer's location or jurisdiction, or the subject

of the interaction, such as the product or service for the transaction. In addition, decisions on customer interactions are guided by a comprehensive view of the customer—their history with the company, current disposition, treatments for similar customers, activities that happen during the interaction and feedback gained from forums, tweets, and other social media channels.

In the current economy, companies have a significant opportunity to differentiate themselves by providing great customer experiences through iBPM.

Optimizing Operations: Benefits for Operators

Leveraging iBPM, organizations can become much more efficient. The various features and capabilities of iBPM help them focus on high-value work. Specifically, iBPM provides the following advantages to operators:

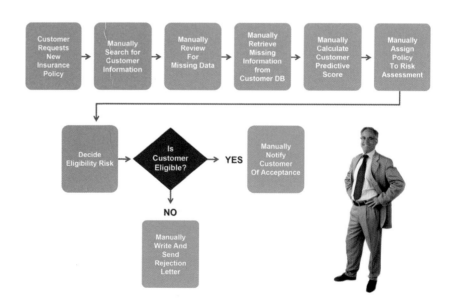

- **Automated Straight-Through Processing:** Traditional work processing involves manual searches, tasks, decisions on business logic, and often paper-based approvals that require chasing paperwork between offices and copying information. Furthermore, traditional work processing often demands toggling between multiple legacy application screens. Through automated processes and policies represented by business rules, iBPM solutions eliminate all this manual activity that increases waste and errors. Furthermore, the intelligence in iBPM can obtain and deliver information at just the right time from multiple sources.

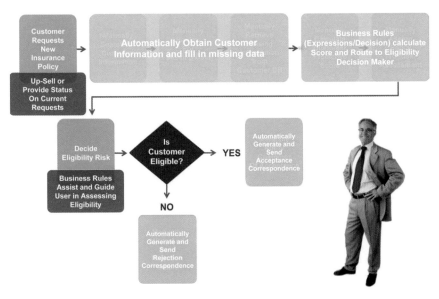

- **Guided Interactions:** For tasks that are assigned to operators, the iBPM suite can actually provide the most relevant, meaningful and guided interaction for the task at hand. Depending on the task and its context, the iBPM-managed interaction can be very simple and intuitive for the operator. With iBPM, the policies and procedures are automated and guide the interaction of the operator or worker. Contrast this to the intense training and often cryptic or complex forms operators typically must deal with to get their jobs done. For example, as the graphics illustrate, without iBPM automation, the process to determine eligibility for an insurance application takes 10 manual steps. With iBPM automation, just-in-time integration, auto-generated correspondence, and iBPM business rules, this process is reduced to only two steps that involve the operator. More importantly, these two steps are processed much more efficiently with the help of automated guidance. Not only has iBPM eliminated eight steps, the remaining two are optimized!
- **Real-Time Process Excellence:** Through iBPM, operations can readily achieve the objectives of process excellence and process optimization. This includes getting rid of waste (Lean) as well as keeping processes in control through avoiding

variance and improving quality (Six Sigma). For example, since the business rules and the processes for managing tasks are automated, the iBPM suite can be "smart" in routing the work to the best resource. Furthermore, the iBPM suite can keep track of service levels and automatically escalate urgencies to keep the processes under control and on time.

- **Next-Best-Action:** Optimizing the customer experience leverages the analytical insight that is mined from data to support decisioning for the customer. This applies to marketing, sales automation, and perhaps most importantly to customer service and support. The sources of the decisioning strategy emanate from business rules that are authored by experts or knowledge workers using predictive models created from data gathered from multiple sources, such as publicly available data, transactional data, or historic data and enterprise data warehouses.

Benefits for the Business

iBPM allows the business to be agile and respond rapidly to manage change in customer and market demands. The response could be through new products, new innovations, and optimized customer experiences. With iBPM, businesses gain enhanced visibility, transparency, and control using the following capabilities:

Other Technologies

| Business Mandate | Requirement Docs | Analysis Docs | Coding | Review | Re-Coding... |

With iBPM

Business Mandate

- **Directly Capturing Business Objectives and Strategies:** In traditional development, the business starts with a mandate, and then uses documentation-heavy tools to capture their requirements. The requirement documents are then used or imported as artifacts with a different tool in order to do a high-level, and then a detailed specification or business analysis. This could result in voluminous documentation, models, or artifacts. At some point, there is a hand-off from business to IT. The business artifacts are then exported and imported into other tools to do technical design. After that, they are exported and imported into yet another tool for coding. With the code, there are continuous reviews and changes. Soon enough, the implementation is completely isolated from the original business requirements. There is no roundtrip, and changes have to go through many tools and phases of export and import. Now, that doesn't inspire agility! This export and import process, and the involvement of so many tools, is the antithesis of managing change with agility.

With iBPM, you are able to directly capture business objectives and measurable business strategies. These are then readily linked to and realized in initiatives that deliver solutions for the business requirements with *zero* coding. To put it in more simple and direct terms: What the business wants to achieve, it can do with minimal loss of meaning, time, or effort in endless translations and mappings between teams and tools. Or in other words, real and practical agility. This ability to directly capture objectives in the iBPM suite is enabled by a rich collection of tools, wizards, and capabilities that tie business goals, use cases, and requirements to actual implementation. Instead of coding, easy to understand forms are used by business and IT, which supports model-driven development.

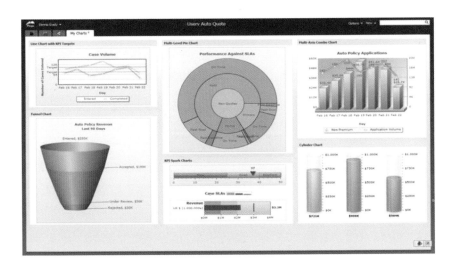

- Measuring Strategies and Monitoring Business Activities: Most enterprises agree that providing solutions and approaches for achieving corporate objectives is important. Yet, in many situations, these measurable strategies fail to be achieved or executed. Dashboards are not enough—you also need to be able to drill down from top-level management objectives to specific processes, organizations, and even individual workers to affect change. In addition, the quantitative monitoring and correction of the business objectives need to be proactive and in real time. Otherwise, performance results lag without a clear link to the executing processes. The more easily you can drill down from management performance to specific executing processes, the better chance there is of aligning business with IT.

As the processes are executed, iBPM keeps track of what you are doing when you are starting a new process instance or a case, and when you are routing work from one participant or operator to another. The system is able to monitor these kinds of activities from various perspectives, whether they are at the application, solution, process, case, operator, or department level. The business is able to monitor all the events and activities that are going on to detect if the process is under control. It makes sure the solution is on par with business objectives. If there are any problems, the iBPM solution will enable businesses to drill down and solve their bottlenecks, all in real time.

- **Owning the Change:** In some organizations, the business is able to own business policies and procedures and make the changes directly, with little to no IT involvement. Business policies, such as when to provide discounts, when to write off a claim, or what constitutes an unacceptable risk, are presented to business users in easy-to-use forms. Similar to desktop applications (such as Microsoft Word® , Excel®, or PowerPoint®), the business can readily make changes to these business rules. If needed, IT could approve the changes to make sure that they do not adversely impact other rules or solutions. The key point here is the empowerment of business users to make changes to the solution directly and "own the change."

- **Providing a Foundation for Business Transformation:** Transformation has many dimensions—innovation, empowering the business to own the change, centers of excellence, globalization, efficiency, and effectiveness to foster great customer experiences—to name a few. The iBPM platform and agile methodologies are transformational because they enable enterprises to rethink and transform all aspects of the business. As the enterprise matures in deploying iBPM solutions, it will be able to achieve a rhythm of change that can keep up with customer expectations, market demands and changing regulations as well as foster cultural changes and innovation. Additionally, iBPM provides the foundation for legacy modernization, by wrapping and renewing home-grown legacy or enterprise resource planning (ERP) point solutions, so that they can be leveraged in agile and transformational intelligent processes and solutions.

Productivity Gains and Other Benefits for IT

Through iBPM, IT can now achieve tremendous productivity gains. If we look at the 60-plus year history of computing, when we went from assembly languages to high-level structured programming languages, such as COBOL, C, PL/I, and so on, we saw enormous productivity gains. Productivity was improved five times to an order of magnitude. When we went from high-level structured programming languages to object-oriented programming languages, such as Simula, Smalltalk, and later C++, Java and C#, we also experienced some productivity gains.

However, when Pegasystems looked for independent studies that evaluated the effectiveness of going from object-oriented programming languages to iBPM as the platform to develop robust applications and solutions, we couldn't find any. So, we commissioned one[10]. We sponsored an objective study, comparing the results for the same business scenario implemented using a state-of-the-art object-oriented programming language and platform and using iBPM. The results were spectacular: Five to seven times more productivity gains using the iBPM suite than the object-oriented programming language. Thus, instead of being a challenge or impediment to IT, iBPM suites actually help IT become more productive and successful.

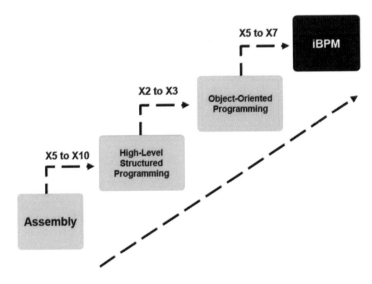

There are additional benefits to IT:

- Unified Platform for Processes, Cases, Rules, and Decisions: Dealing with one unified platform and solution with a single, easy-to-use and consistent interface for building solutions is a tremendous benefit for IT. The importance of this cannot be overstated. Traditionally, business rules and process management have not been unified into one core iBPM platform that can be used by both business users and IT. Usually, rules and processes are kept separate. Trying to align business and IT by creating artificial boundaries and roles to fit multiple products is not a great recipe for success.

---

[10] You can find the white paper of the productivity study, "Capgemini Pega BPM vs Eclipse Java IDE", at http://www.pega.com/resources/capgemini-pega-bpm-vs-eclipse-java-ide

Logically, rules and processes should be modeled and executed within the same system. It makes much better sense to think about, analyze, abstract, and model the declarative rules in conjunction with the information model, the organization model, the workflows, and the user interactions. The appropriate use of business rules changes the topology of a process flow. It also simplifies the flow and facilitates the management of applications. Situational policies can also be used to define when one should use a particular flow, a particular business rule, a trading partner, or a back-end application. The policies are applied in many situations, both within processes and across applications. Business and IT need a common, consistent language for processes and business rules. This can only happen if the two are unified within one complete iBPM platform. The very essence of iBPM is to have one unified platform with the same metadata and core engine, and a single point for maintenance and revisions.

- **Enterprise iBPM Repository:** Directly related to the benefits of a unified platform is the value of a unified repository. With the unified and cohesive iBPM platform, IT is able to achieve tremendous productivity leveraging the dynamic, multi-dimensional repository of the iBPM system. This is a single repository that maintains all of the processes, case types, business rules, decisions, UI, and integration. It thus becomes the foundation for change and reuse. In collaboration with the business, IT can create new solutions by easily customizing and extending the reusable assets, while adding layers of specialization for specific customers, geographical locations, new lines of business, or new functions, for example.

- **Successful SOA through iBPM:** The road to success for service-oriented architecture (SOA) initiatives runs through iBPM. There are many reasons for this. iBPM allows IT to focus and prioritize the services that need to support business solutions with real business value. iBPM methodologies also help IT to think big while starting small. iBPM is both a service consumer as well as service producer. It can create composite applications and publish them as services. There is a division of labor between higher level iBPM functions and features and lower-level SOA infrastructure capabilities, especially the enterprise service bus. Lower-level SOA plumbing technologies can be leveraged for brokering service calls. The business focus for SOA, while leveraging underlying plumbing technologies, is critical. Business and IT must align themselves around iBPM solutions that have business objectives, inherent business object models and the associated processes, business rules, usage models, and integration necessary to achieve concrete results while leveraging various infrastructure technologies like SOA. This approach allows organizations to deploy best-practice processes and rules in weeks—rather than months—and build the process improvement momentum.

iBPM for the Enterprise

To wrap up, if we look at iBPM in the enterprise ecosystem, the business will have business objectives and measurable strategies to achieve. iBPM is both the source and the monitor of these objectives, able to observe them continuously and in real time. Often the business strategies are expressed through Key Performance Indicators (KPIs), following strategic methodologies such as the balanced scorecard or NPS. Some KPIs need to be optimized and handled through a continuous improvement methodology like Lean or Six Sigma. Empowered with iBPM, the business can continuously examine its activities, effect immediate change, and try to optimize its strategies to achieve the business objectives. The key point is that whether you are optimizing certain aspects of your critical-to-quality measures, or you are trying to improve the performance of your KPIs, the foundation is iBPM. iBPM is the transformational platform that helps organizations keep processes in control, innovate with new solutions, and continuously improve *in real time.*

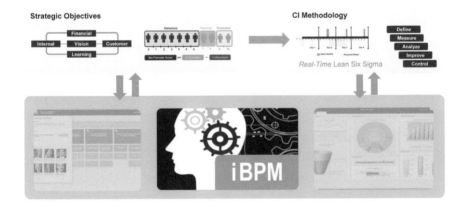

Example: Insurance Organization Delivers Staggering Global Results

Vision: One of the leading property-casualty and general insurance organizations has been an innovator in leveraging advanced iBPM technology throughout the enterprise for the last decade. The company's management team decided that a new comprehensive approach to claims management was needed worldwide. The existing methods were not producing consistent results for the enterprise or the customer. Many challenges needed to be overcome to deliver on the vast promise of a single claims management approach that would span the company's global operations.

Solution: The insurance organization launched a major initiative to capitalize on its vision and to fully leverage the organization's global reach. The company used iBPM to deliver a single worldwide platform that would allow them to institutionalize 90 years of claims management experience. iBPM's scalable architecture, combined with a strong governance model, provided the right platform to help the project succeed. The company leveraged iBPM's rules-based technology to create a configurable, claims-process core that is designed to be reused across the global enterprise. This inherent flexibility has proven to be the strength of the deployment.

Results: Business results confirm the competitive benefits of the global claims solution. Claims handling cycle times have been reduced by 30% and adjusters can now expedite claims to the "right resource, right time" to deliver the optimal claim outcome. A 10 point reduction in combined ratio for individual lines of business has been achieved, along with a substantial reduction in expenses associated with global claim leakage. Robust claims case management automates processes designed to mitigate loss potential, delivering a 5+% reduction in indemnity expense. Furthermore, enhancements in adjudication accuracy have delivered a much higher return on investment (ROI) than originally forecasted.

CHAPTER 3

How Can You Succeed With Intelligent BPM?

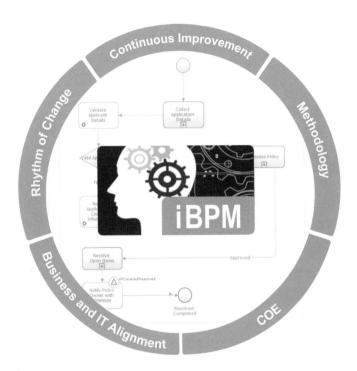

In this chapter, we examine how enterprises—how you—can succeed with iBPM. As the diagram illustrates, there are a number of components for achieving success with an iBPM. The iBPM technology and platform are necessary for success, but they alone are not sufficient. Like any other technology, it needs to be understood and applied systematically to achieve success. Unlike other technologies, iBPM has a robust organizational impact. It changes to the core how enterprises build and deploy solutions. This change can come incrementally, starting with one iBPM project, and then radiate to others. Human nature and, by proxy, traditional organizational behavior, resists change. However, by "thinking big" and "starting small," with demonstrable results, organizations can greatly enhance their chances of success.

The essential elements of iBPM improvement must be carefully followed to guarantee success and ensure a positive transformational effect on the organization. iBPM is becoming a means to finally narrow the execution gaps that develop when change management objectives outpace the implementation by IT, which can damage profitability and customer satisfaction. Take a scenario common to almost every large organization. You have an offsite meeting where the executive team lists its organizational objectives and goals. These are used to create budgets and plans for line-of-business managers and IT to execute. Executives expect these organizations to implement the objectives with zeal and excitement. Typically, after a few months, it becomes evident that realizing the corporate objectives will be difficult. Due to changing market conditions and customer expectations, organizations are finding it hard to stay on course with their original plans and objectives.

Organizations need to deal with exceptions and uncertainty on a daily basis. They need to respond quickly to change, and change is coming faster than ever. This is where iBPM can come to the rescue. More than any other platform or tool, we constantly hear of tangible results achieved through iBPM deployments. Why? As we saw in Chapter 1, iBPM focuses on the business and helps the organization eliminate the execution gaps, promoting productivity and customer-centricity throughout the enterprise.

There are three key elements to successfully using iBPM in your organization:

- A focus on the business objectives
- A continuous improvement methodology
- Commitment to a Center of Excellence

Focusing on Business Objectives

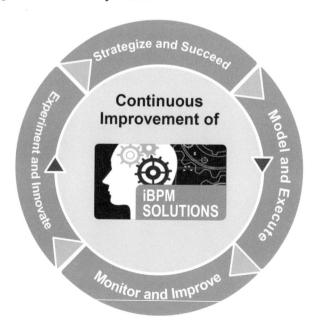

Business users have the best knowledge of their business processes and business rules. If you want your IT department to effectively communicate with business, you need them to build iBPM applications that directly reflect the business owner's understanding of the desired business policies and procedures. The overall cycle can be described as follows:

- **Strategize and Succeed:** Business objectives provide the overall directive of the enterprise, such as penetrating specific markets or improving social marketing. Strategies support these overall business objectives. Typically, there will be specific KPIs to measure the success of the chosen strategic initiatives. The objectives and the strategies focus on the *What.* The iBPM improvement  technologies and initiatives operationalize the improvements and focus on the *How.* So what is being executed for improvement? The process flows, the dynamic cases, and the accompanying business rules and decisions. With iBPM, the business objectives, the strategies, as well as the various execution initiatives are all captured in one unified platform. The success, measured in profit, ROI, increased customer satisfaction and other measures, should be immediately visible. This is important: IT and business owners should agree on what would constitute an improvement through the elimination of manual tasks and automation of business rules.
- **Model and Execute:** Business users should be able to easily design processes and author the rules that are associated with decision steps, service level agreements, or constraints within the processes. iBPM is a model-driven development platform which simply means what you model is what you *execute,* versus simply generating modeling artifacts or documentation. As noted in the previous chapter, the import/export of models between various tools should be avoided. One of the keys to creating business-focused solutions and enabling continuous improvement is to make sure all types of authors who are creating business rules are using the same environment and platform, whether they are business stakeholders, analysts, or IT developers. This should be accompanied by an ability to roll changes back in case there are problems. In other words, versioning and configuration management should be built in with modeling and design. Using this approach, iBPM brings IT and business together to collaborate and rapidly deploy iBPM applications via incremental and iterative changes.
- **Monitor and Analyze:** As soon as iBPM applications are deployed, they can be monitored. Business measures can be viewed and analyzed through a "pull" of real-time, or historical and analytical reports. iBPM stakeholders can author rules that determine what to watch for and what actions to take if there are potential bottlenecks. Through real-time monitoring of activities, the business gains complete visibility and control of automated processes, enabling business

owners to drill down and affect change in real time. As we shall see in the next chapter, analysis can be further improved as iBPM is able to learn from historical data and operationalize predictive models as well as continuously learn and adapt through adaptive models.

- Innovate and Experiment: Through innovation, organizations can create new services and products that help their customers, partners, and of course, the organization's bottom line. In fact, given the pace of change, innovation becomes essential for survival. iBPM is critical to helping organizations quickly invent because it allows new applications or changes to existing applications to be piloted and experimented with before they are put into production. Piloting allows the organization to analyze any potential issues in the overall implementation of the processes. For instance, the solution could be deployed on a smaller scale with fewer people. After experimentation, enhancements could be introduced for mass deployment. Sometimes, the experimentation can involve simulation which is statistical and data-based, or a simulation of technical integration components that could be built subsequently. Real-world experiential feedback is essential to the success of any project. Once ratified, the pilot can then be immediately rolled out for deployment on a larger scale.

Continuous Improvement Methodology

iBPM agile methodology is the most important requirement for success and continuous improvement[11]. Because continuous improvement is the essence and core of the iBPM methodology, the best way to reap the benefits of iBPM is to operate in the context of the continuous improvement lifecycle. This means constantly monitoring, piloting, quickly
deploying, and profiting. It also means eliminating bottlenecks through the design and deployment of iBPM applications. A continuous improvement methodology specifies the roles, phases, project management, and iterations of solutions.

Center of Excellence

As iBPM becomes more and more pervasive, it is imperative for both large and mid-sized enterprises to establish an iBPM Center of Excellence (COE) that focuses on

---

[11] We will discuss this in greater depth in Chapter 10.

the deployment of successful iBPM projects.[12] (COEs are also called Centers of Competency (COC) or Competency Centers (CC)). The COE has many functions:

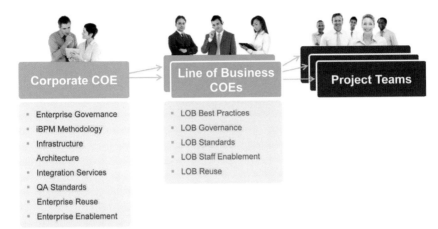

- The iterative COE methodology identifies the participants, artifacts, and phases of iBPM projects.
- COE governance of iBPM projects identifies the policies for roles, standards, decision making, and deliverables.
- The COE also attempts to provide the guidelines and models for building reusable corporate assets captured in process and policy models, supervise iBPM methodology execution, and enable the staff involved in the iBPM projects.

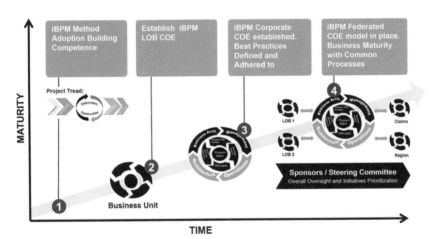

---

[12] An iterative, iBPM-enabled methodology is a crucial part of the overall transformational roadmap with iBPM and will be discussed in detail in Chapter 10. Establishing and governing the methodology lays the foundation for the iBPM COE.

Typically, the enterprise will have a corporate level COE, which will work closely with multiple line-of-business (LOB) COEs and their iBPM project teams. At the corporate or enterprise level, the COE governs enterprise standards as well as focuses on integration and infrastructure standards. The LOB COEs focus on business standards and best practices. In the iBPM journey, an organization will often start with an LOB project, and it is highly recommended to launch a LOB COE as soon as possible. Over time, the LOB COE can grow to a corporate iBPM COE and eventually a federated iBPM COE, especially in large and global organizations.

The iBPM COE promotes best practices for continuous improvement lifecycles through an iBPM maturity model, which is a roadmap that helps evolve the COE guidelines through iBPM engineering, adoption, and governance.

COE Governance

No initiative can succeed without governance. There are five major categories of governance in robust iBPM COEs.

1. Reuse and Customization of the Enterprise Repository of Corporate Assets: The corporate asset policies deal with the enterprise repository governance. Process solutions involving information, flow, business rules, case types, integration, predictive models, and user interfaces can be reused within and across functional units. The COE needs to establish the structure for creating reusable assets. iBPM assets can be reused at both the corporate and LOB COE levels, and typically there will be considerable sharing and customization of assets across LOB COEs.
2. Enablement: Promotion, Training, and Certification of iBPM Development Talent: The COE oversees staffing, enablement, and training policies that govern the required competencies, experience, and certifications of the team implementing and maintaining the iBPM solution.
3. Project Management: Project management policies are perhaps the best understood, focusing on iterations, schedules, resources, and cost governance. The project managers deploy and govern agile methodologies for continuous improvement.
4. Modern Business Architecture: This includes business performance management, analytics, master data governance, the technical service-oriented architecture, and the overall cloud deployment strategies.
5. Enterprise Digitization Governance: Digitization of the enterprise is a significant trend that is transforming businesses. Digitization technologies include cloud computing, social networking, mobile devices, and analytics. Digitization needs governance and a strategic roadmap within the context of iBPM solutions.

Succeeding with iBPM

So, how do you succeed with iBPM? First, by aligning business and IT to speak the same language of modeled and automated policies and procedures. Chapter 2 discussed key values of iBPM that benefit both business and IT—measurable strategies, unified policies and procedures, extensible solution frameworks, and accessible platforms. Leveraging these capabilities, business and IT can speak the same language of policies and procedures using different types of business rules such as decisioning, constraints, expressions, event correlation rules, and service levels. iBPM also enables business processes, information and organization models to be communicated, developed, and deployed with zero coding—all of which helps business and IT understand each other.

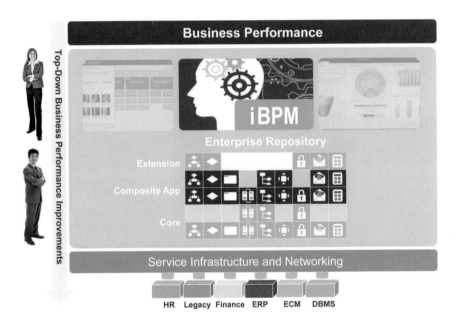

Second, you can achieve a rhythm of change through continuous improvement. Business focuses on performance objectives such as increased revenue, additional market share, new markets, cost savings, innovation, and compliance. IT focuses on reliable infrastructure. iBPM is the platform that handles top-down business objectives to generate increased business value, while leveraging the underlying infrastructure, which facilitates rapid change and a continuous improvement cycle. KPIs are realized through automated policies and procedures in iBPM. Both real-time business activity monitoring and historic data warehouses are used to compare benchmarks of KPIs and potentially introduce changes to policies and procedures.

Third, governing projects with an iBPM COE and a methodology that is iterative and agile promotes best practices, sharing and reuse, and clear rules, policies, procedures, and roadmaps that lead to successful implementations.

Pitfalls That Prevent iBPM Success

iBPM projects can fail. Even with the best of intentions, maturing iBPM COEs, and robust iBPM methodologies, there are pitfalls that can prohibit large-scale, transformational deployment of iBPM. This section summarizes the seven common pitfalls that prevent iBPM success:

- Not Securing Executive-Level Support: iBPM is transformational and often involves and effects mission-critical solutions with human participants. Because it can be a real game changer that empowers workers, organizations need to involve an executive business sponsor from the very beginning of the project. Without executive support, the project is likely to fail.
- Selecting the Wrong Projects: Many business process initiatives fail because the team takes on a project that is very important to the business, but is too complex or risky, or does not leverage the strengths of iBPM technology. Worse, it could be a combination of both. So, finding a balance between complexity, risk, and business value is essential for success.
- Neglecting to Form a Sustainable iBPM Team: This relates to the roles in the LOB or corporate iBPM COE. Simply acquiring some iBPM training and then going forth with an iBPM project is a recipe for disaster. Companies fail at revamping their business process practices because a robust and enabled iBPM team is not put in place.
- Analysis Paralysis: iBPM is about business process *automation*. iBPM solutions can achieve quick wins and immediate operational results that either generate new revenue or cut costs, or both. Companies often get mesmerized by "what-if" simulation models, and spend weeks analyzing the "perfect" models. Companies

often miss market opportunities that are offered by an agile iBPM development approach with tangible results and immediate customer benefits because they become too focused on creating the perfect modeling artifacts.

- **Ripping and Replacing Legacy Applications and Technology:** Organizations need to view modernization as a journey, with incremental steps towards full deployment of iBPM solutions for all mission-critical and support processes. While in some cases, it might make sense for a company with a huge IT wallet and vast resources to embark on a new technological journey, these companies often sink countless dollars and resources into ripping and replacing an entire system in "big bang" projects. For iBPM, the mantra should always be "Think big, but start small." It is far better is to incrementally wrap, modernize, and renew legacy systems for tangible and incremental results.

- **Failure to "Own the Change":** As noted above, iBPM is about continuous improvement. The "own the change" value proposition involves both business and IT. For success, the business should be intimately involved in owning the change. The COE guidelines should provide the best practices, knowledge transfer, expertise, experience, guidance, and reusable assets to improve the success of project teams and of the enterprise.

- **Fear of Transformation:** iBPM could be the most important catalyst for transforming the organization—but keep in mind that human nature resists change. During the industrial revolution, many workers lost their jobs due to automation. iBPM is currently transforming the white collar service industry, and some jobs will be lost, while others will be significantly changed. Not every organization is ready to place all their bets on iBPM, so it is wise to implement iBPM maturity levels incrementally. While enterprise transformation as a concept seems overwhelming, it becomes obtainable when it is broken into tangible and successful phases over time.

Example: Center of Excellence in Financial Services

Vision: One of the largest financial service companies in the United States established a Center of Excellence (CoE) to accelerate iBPM implementations and maturity. The goal was to eliminate development silos and improve the quality of project design and implementation. The functions of the CoE team include bridging the gaps between IT and business; integrating process reengineering and continuous improvement into iBPM projects; centralizing and reusing application code and assets; creating and maintaining architectural standards; and promoting standard methodologies, tools and education.

Solution: Housed within the central technology and operations organization, the CoE interacts with every line of business (LOB), providing consulting services internally. With a focus on process and governance, the CoE works closely with the LOB's business and technical staff to help them make sure each project is a good fit for iBPM, develop a sound business case and ROI, determine where process re-engineering is desirable, and ensure the team has the right training.

One of the key initiatives for the CoE was to build a foundation of reusable assets that includes a downloadable component of code for class structures, rule sets and other application assets, such as interfaces to legacy systems. As the CoE matures, it will continue to strengthen design, code, and pre-flight reviews as well as develop better ways to measure how well a project delivers on the expected goals.

Results: Because of the reusable assets foundation created by the CoE, the company has saved hundreds of initial build hours. The focus on design and build governance through the pre-flight reviews has significantly increased guardrail compliance, making applications easier to maintain and eliminating performance issues. In addition, with project participants properly trained, standardization, and use of an agile, iterative project methodology, go-live time for projects has been reduced by weeks. And hundreds of maintenance hours have been saved by using specialized CoE development resources to conduct quarterly enterprise system analysis and asset updates.

CHAPTER 4

Business Rules and Analytics for the "i" in iBPM

At this point, it should be obvious that iBPM is strategic as it forms the core of the modern enterprise business architecture. In this chapter we focus on the most important aspects of the "i" in iBPM. In addition to *intelligence*, the "i" also stands for *intent*—what the iBPM solution or a party and participant in a case, process or task is trying to achieve. In other words, what is the objective of the action? The intelligence understood about the situation needs to be analyzed, captured, and then operationalized in *decisions* to achieve the intent.

Business Rules

As noted in Chapter 1, there are many sources of policies within organizations. These sources include policy and procedure manuals, the heads of subject matter experts or knowledge workers, and data sources. All of these policies and procedures contain *business rules*. Business rules have many definitions and connotations, but, essentially business rules are policies, constraints, or practices and business guidance that need to be followed. Business rules are ubiquitous—the business declares the rules and expects them to be followed. Here are some examples of business rules:

- Example 1: Categorizing Risk
    - IF Current Balance is < $500 AND Customer has a good credit THEN Low Risk

- Example 2: Expression
    - The Tax calculation is a function of the state, amount, and product type

- Example 3: Constraint
    - The amount of vacation requested should be always less or equal to the amount accrued

- Example 4: Event Correlation
    - If Shipment arrived AND PO has been approved THEN send delivery notice

Business rules are "declarative." What does that mean? With declarative thinking, your focus is on declaring your intention, not the implementation details of the rule. Declarative means independent from the time, method, or order of execution. The focus is on the business logic. As noted above, in most businesses, business rules are enacted through various documents, and these can even be company memos sent to announce new policies or changes to existing policies. For example, a memo states that from now on all customer complaint correspondence needs to be forwarded to a complaint task force; or that starting 10/1/2014 any type of purchase exceeding $5,000 needs *two* levels of approval. These are examples of business rule declarations. No matter how or where they are implemented, the rules must be followed and executed.

Business rules can be associated with a process or shared across processes. There are many types of rules that can be used in conjunction with processes. Some of these declarative rules could apply to the process as a whole. For example, you can have a rule action (e.g. escalate or inform owner) for implementing service level agreements (SLAs) and associated with the entire case. Other rules could be associated with specific activities, such as the decision as to who should be assigned a task at a particular step.

Within the topology of the process there will be decision points, typically represented with a diamond shape. Behind this diamond shape you can have decision trees or tables which are evaluated, and the result of this evaluation then helps select one (or more) of the branches emanating from the diamond shape.

Situation

— World Card
— Gold Customer

Write-Off?

No   **Yes**

If...
— <u>Dispute Amount</u> is less than $51
— AND <u>Transaction</u> is not disputed as a fraudulent transaction
— AND <u>Customer</u> has disputed less than two transactions this year

Then...
YES. Fully credit the customer without even initiating the dispute
(i.e., Write-off the transaction)

For example, a business rule which is a decision tree can drive the decision of writing off a disputed credit card claim. The purpose of the rule is to decide whether to write off the claim ("Yes") or not ("No"). It uses three conditions:

- The amount of the dispute
- The potential fraudulence (which could depend on other rules), and
- The history of the customer (has not disputed more than two in a year).

This example also includes the circumstance or the "situation" of rules. This particular decision tree rule is applied when the type of credit card product is "World" and the category of the customer is "Gold". The rule is applied only in this context. There will be many other rules with the same purpose ("Write off?") but for different situations or circumstances, spanning different types of products or customers. For instance, all the other constraints being the same, for Silver customers, the rule might write off disputes less than $25 and not the $51 for Gold customers. In the iBPM solution, all the assets—including decision rules—are organized along a number of dimensions (type of product or service, category of customer, geographical location, etc.), and then iBPM applies the most appropriate rule based on the situation or context of the process execution.

Business Insight from Business Data for Business Decisions

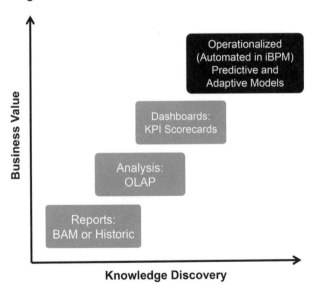

The "i" in iBPM also stands for *insight* that is obtained (or mined) from data. Data can be historic or real time (transactional). It can be structured, as in relational tables, or unstructured, as in text. Data can come from a single application or a single source, or it can come from multiple applications or sources. Data can be private or public. It can be from any enterprise solutions that generate data such as customer interactions, service provisioning, support processes, or just about any function in the organization. Today, enterprises generate hundreds of exabytes[13] of content annually. There is also the potential large insight from big data to make recommendations based on the behavior of customers. Big data is characterized by large volume and variety and changes with increasing velocity. The question is: Are we gaining insight or knowledge from the data that we are constantly generating? More importantly, are we operationalizing this insight in business processes?

In the illustration, as you go right on the X-axis, you have better and better insight or knowledge discovery. On the Y-axis, as you go up, you have better and better business value. As illustrated here, there are a number of analytical techniques and tools that are associated with business intelligence (BI). These cover various capabilities, or aspects of insight or knowledge discovery, and business value. At the bottom left, you have business activity monitoring (BAM) reports or historic reports. Then, you have online analytical processing (OLAP). With more business value and insight, you have KPIs and scorecards. At the top right, you have data mining and "operationalized" predictive as well as adaptive models. This operationalization is achieved through *intelligent* BPM.

Enterprise Performance Management

This brings us back to "B," the "business" in iBPM that we touched upon in Chapter 1. There are many dimensions and aspects of the "B" in iBPM. One of these aspects is reflected in business objectives or KPIs as we examined in Chapter 2, such as gaining additional market share, increasing revenue, decreasing risk or cost, with specific and measurable results.

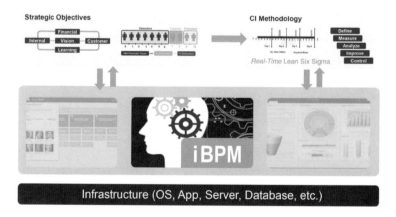

---

[13] An exabyte is a billion gigabytes.

Some of these KPIs could undergo continuous improvement methodology cycles, such as Lean and Six Sigma. Lean focuses on reducing waste and increasing process efficiency. Six Sigma focuses on reducing variance and improving the quality of the processes. Now, the KPIs that are measured and improved through a continuous improvement methodology could correspond to properties that pertain to an iBPM solution or application. That is, the Lean and Six Sigma continuous improvement methodologies are improving efficiencies of processes that are automated through iBPM. Such continuous improvement or Lean Six Sigma initiatives become iBPM projects[14]. The process will be kept under control in real time.

The business objectives can also be monitored and controlled through an enterprise performance management dashboard. Here, you might be dealing with data warehouses or historic data, where iBPM solutions are one of the sources that are providing information to the warehouse. In addition, iBPM provides out-of-the-box, real-time business activity monitoring that allows stakeholders to act on potential bottlenecks in real time. Whether you are dealing with real-time reports, historic data, or you have a continuous improvement methodology, the point is that all of these measures emanate from properties, or the performance of solutions that are automated and deployed through the iBPM.

Contextual and Situational Intelligence

When business applications execute, there is always a context or business intent—the type of the customer, the location or jurisdiction of the customer, or the specific business product—to name a few. All these dimensions need to be used to select and provide the best policy, user interaction, or information source for a given situation. Through robust iBPM solutions, the adaptive enterprise needs to reflect the way people manage change in their organization. Businesses need to treat customers uniquely, based on a particular set of criteria. iBPM can provide the context and specific solutions for their specific customers or lines of business. The iBPM platform—especially its enterprise repository of business rules and processes, dynamic case types, decisions, UI, and integration—needs to support optimized reuse and specialization, and then the automatic selection of the most appropriate specialized asset (policy or procedure) for the given situation.

Using iBPM, enterprises should be able to adapt by easily reusing and globally specializing their business assets. The assets are iBPM assets for execution including flow fragments, business rules of different types (decision, constraint, expression), UI, information, integration, etc. The multi-dimensional organization of iBPM assets is the mechanism that enables the enterprise to adapt easily to:

---

[14] Real-Time Lean Six Sigma is covered in Chapter 8.

- Introduce changes as deltas that capture specific policy or procedure changes.
- Customize and specialize so that, for instance, different customers are treated differently, depending upon who they are, where they are, what type of product/service they are requesting, when the request is made, etc.
- Organize solutions for optimal reuse across the enterprise and then specialize for specific locations, customer categories, solution frameworks, or lines of businesses.

Think of giving special discounts for specific types of customers. The discount calculation is a specialization and it depends upon the type of the customer. It could also depend upon specific jurisdictions, locations or timeframe. That is how business manages specializations and that is exactly how an iBPM should manage change.

Predictive iBPM

While many business processes are about doing things the right way, there is not always the same emphasis on doing the right things. Referring to a popular theme in this day and age, there may be a near-optimal process in place to fulfill a mortgage application, but should the mortgage have been approved in the first place? What's the probability of default, and what is the expected loss to the company? Similarly, all the sales fulfillment processes may be running full throttle, but are the right products being offered—those that, in the end, maximize the lifetime value of that customer? Should a different product have been proposed, at a different price, or with a different incentive?

This is where predictive analytics comes into play. Businesses have many hidden treasures in their data. The data can be held in operational databases, data warehouses or even census or publicly available data. There is value in the individual data sources, but even more so in their combination. Customer purchase patterns, satisfaction drivers, and future behavior are all "hidden" in this data. The whole purpose of, and motivation for, predictive analytics is to discover these patterns (predictive models), use them to predict future behavior, and then act on the insight.

Prediction is ubiquitous. Almost every business flow or business rule has some element of prediction in it. Most of the time, requirements arise from intuition, history, experience, or ad-hoc mechanisms to capture policies and procedures. Sometimes the original reasons for enacting these policies have long been obsolete. In contrast, predictive modeling is a scientific discipline within data mining that uses measurable *predictors* to predict the behavior of customers. These predictors can be an ordinal or numerical value that can be predicted from other variable values. Historical data is analyzed and modeled to predict future behavior. Examples of predictors include purchasing preferences, geographical location, age, income, and properties pertaining to the history of activities. Predictive models can be discovered from either operational data or data warehouses. Per the mortgage example, without predictive insight many decisions will be bad decisions. It's surprising how many bad decisions are made based on hope, gut feel, mere assumptions, or a naïve interpretation of historic trends. Where customers, who are notably fickle, are concerned, it's almost always impossible to play by ear. Advances in statistical analysis and machine learning have made it possible in many cases to predict customer behavior with a high level of accuracy. Moreover, it is possible to calculate the confidence one can have in those predictions. There's no more guess work in trying to figure out the right thing to do. And for every possible action, you'll know the margin of error in advance.

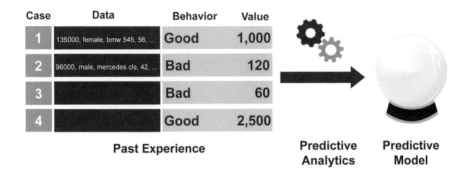

Case	Data	Behavior	Value
1	135000, female, bmw 545, 56, ...	Good	1,000
2	96000, male, mercedes cls, 42, ...	Bad	120
3		Bad	60
4		Good	2,500

Past Experience · Predictive Analytics · Predictive Model

So the main philosophy of predictive iBPM is to aggregate and mine historic operational data (and sometimes publicly available data) in order to make predictions about behaviors, and then use these predictions within operations automated through iBPM solutions.

Adaptive iBPM

Companies that have automated decisions as part of their iBPM solution can, in some circumstances, opt for a system of continuous learning and adaptation within the system itself. Any organization that is responsibly using static predictive models will want to ensure that those models are continuously monitored. They need to know when the historic data used for modeling is no longer representative of current circumstances. In that case, the model will get 'tired' and needs to be replaced by a new model based on more recent data. With traditional predictive analytics, once the predictive model has been inferred from the data, it will not change anymore. The model is derived from a snapshot of the data and immutable afterwards. There are many circumstances where this is acceptable and some where it is even desirable. An altogether different approach is using so-called adaptive (or self-learning) models. Instead of looking at a snapshot of data, this model looks at a moving window of data as it enters the adaptive system. Such adaptable predictive[15] models are always up to date and never get tired. If the quality (i.e. predictive power) of adaptive predictive models versus static predictive models is comparable, it would seem that adaptive models are the better option. Adaptive and self-learning analytics can be leveraged to automatically adjust, for example, to market and customer dynamics depending on what is happening with the markets or the customers. The illustration shows the benefits of predictive and adaptive iBPM.

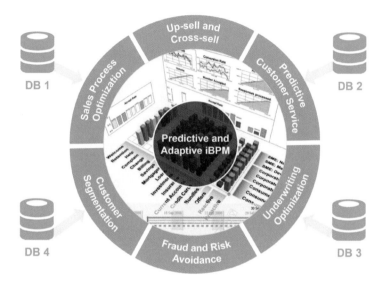

A popular use is where iBPM solutions are used in the CRM or marketing space, and the decision strategy adapts to changes in customer behavior or market dynamics. Customer behavior can change because of demographic trends, legislation, interest rates, or a myriad of other factors. Similarly, competitive offers or pricing can stir up things and impact how customers behave. Rather than trying to re-calibrate predictive models manually—forever testing when such models get less accurate, then developing updated versions—adaptive systems will update automatically without human intervention.

This capability is available in domains where the link between decisions and the feedback about the quality of those decisions is unambiguous and the time lag relatively short. That is, it's possible to give the system a slap on the wrist when it makes a bad decision (or reward it for a good decision), and the slap follows the bad decision in quick order. In such domains (and there are many that qualify outside CRM and marketing), the iBPM solution becomes proactive, not reactive as is typically the case. It's one thing to effectively measure that change is needed,

---

[15] Vs. static predictive (often used as a synonym for predictive).

and then be able to make that change in an agile manner. It's quite another to fully automate this process and have the improvements implemented by a self-learning, adaptive system.

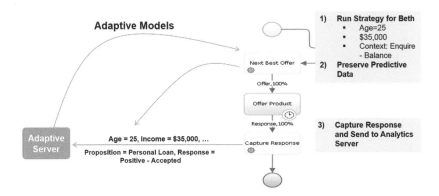

From Business Intelligence to Intelligent BPM

iBPM solutions can adapt or change the various recommendations they give to customer service representatives, such as recommendations for up-selling, cross-selling, predictive customer service, optimizing underwriting rules, fraud and risk avoidance, treating different customers differently, or sales process optimizations.

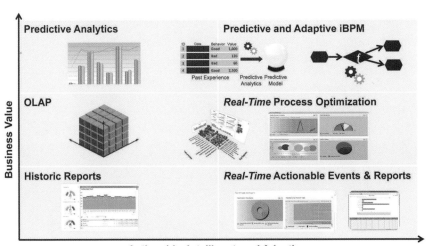

We put all of these concepts together in this rather busy illustration. You want your solutions, in the combination of this dynamic between iBPM and business intelligence, to be actionable and adaptive. This is represented by the X-axis. You also want to have as much business value as possible. This is represented by the

Y-axis[16]. You can take actions from historic reports, data warehouses, or data marts with online analytical processing. You can also take action by performing predictive analytics on historic data. As you go to the right, you deal with real-time iBPM data. You can have real-time actionable reports, where business owners can find out what is going on in their organizations and immediately take action, and even define business rules to take actions. You can do real-time process optimizations by mining the process data. When it comes to the actionable and adaptive dimension, as well as optimized business value, the most promising aspect of the dynamic in iBPM is represented on the top upper-right hand corner as predictive and adaptive iBPM.

---

[16] This is similar to the Business value–Knowledge Discovery we saw earlier, but here with special emphasis on the actionable and adaptive.

Example: Handling Customers Intelligently

Vision: An international bank wanted to provide an exceptional experience at the account opening process. The bank believed that the relationship had to start off well, as the first 90 days of a banking relationship is when 70% of all extended business with clients typically occurs. Navigating through manual processes on the dozens of screens in numerous legacy systems just to create a new account was making the customer's first experience with the bank a painful one. The bank set out to design a new account opening system that would provide a fast, simple, and engaging experience while gathering data from the customer.

Solution: The international bank found the advanced technology it was looking for with iBPM. Its iBPM-enabled solution enabled the bank's client advisors to share their screens, directly interacting with their clients, and showcasing their world-class system. The system integrated tens of legacy systems, intelligently automated over 150 processes for account

 opening, and enabled the bank to gather information about its customers. Beginning with account opening, predictive analytics contextually make recommendations to clients at every step of the relationship. These helpful recommendations create a more meaningful relationship for the customer as the individual now feels the bank knows them personally and not as just another body.

Results: The bank saw its relationship opening time reduced from 25 to 15 minutes. The pleasant first experience and consistently personable relationship realized a 10% lift in additional product sales and a 50% increase in activation for add-on services. In just 12 months, there was a 40% increase in the company's Net Promoter Score relative to its competition. The bank was able to create a customer experience that clients shared with friends, family, and colleagues. The bank used iBPM to redefine the banking relationship and create an environment where they could build customer relationships that would last.

CHAPTER 5

The Road to SOA Success Runs through iBPM

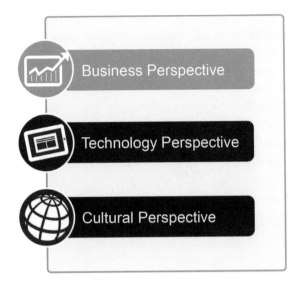

In this chapter, we turn our attention to the service infrastructure and focus on the relationship between service-oriented architectures (SOA) and iBPM. We would like to do that in the context of service-oriented enterprises (SOEs)[17]. SOEs are enterprises[18] that see themselves as service producers or providers, as well as service consumers. There are actually three perspectives of service-oriented enterprises: a business perspective, a technological perspective, and perhaps most importantly, a cultural perspective.

Business Perspective of SOE

As we discussed in Chapter 1 and illustrated here, the "B" in iBPM contains KPIs and business objectives. These could be tied to automated and executing business process applications. The "B" also covers business requirements, which can be captured directly in the iBPM solution. The "B" helps business innovation, as well as business change and agility, all realized through the iBPM system.

---

[17] For more information on *Service-Oriented Enterprises*, see my book on http://www.pega.com/featured/soe%20, or on Amazon.com.
[18] Service-Oriented Enterprises are also Adaptive Enterprises, but the focus here is on the relationship between SOA and iBPM.

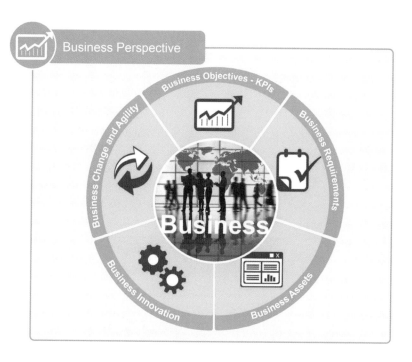

The organization pursues business objectives, specific measurable strategies supporting these objectives, and underlying business performance measures for these, either from data warehouses or business activity monitoring of iBPM-based applications. This gives the business strategic measures for overall enterprise performance management and business performance dashboards, where the business attempts to gain insight and act upon data that is obtained from historic as well as real-time activity monitoring of the applications built with iBPM.

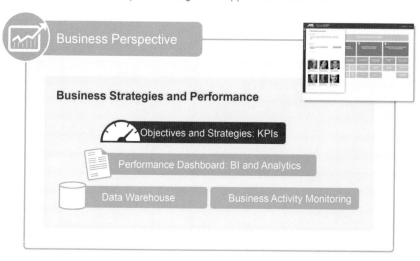

Technological Perspectives

At the other end of the spectrum, you have SOAs with a technology perspective. SOA is actually an architectural pattern that involves a "loose coupling" of service providers and service consumers.

- Loose Coupling: This means that you can use the service and integrate it within your application, while at the same time you are isolated from the details of the service's implementation language, platform, location, or status. SOA entails the reuse of services. So, once certain aspects of the application programming interfaces of services are exposed and a "contract" is defined, they could be invoked through a service producer-service consumer interaction. This provides a lot of flexibility for service connectivity within the enterprise as well as between trading partners.
- Standards Based: SOA tends to be standards-based. This is especially true with web services standards, such as SOAP, WSDL, and WS-Security. Increasingly, organizations are using the REST (Representational State Transfer) architectural style for service interactions. SOA through SOAP is based on XML and is quite verbose and complex. There are many standards associated with SOAP for security, reliability, transactions, and more. SOA through REST is much simpler and relies on readily available standards, such as HTTP and JSON[19] as well as HTML or XML. REST architectural style can potentially provide the same level of security and reliability as SOA through SOAP standards. Furthermore, many mobile devices and cloud services leverage REST for their apps.

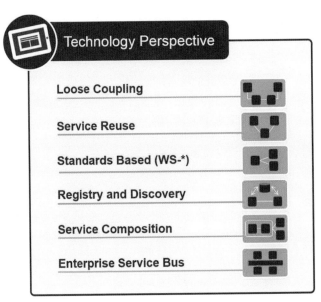

---

[19] http://www.json.org/

- **Registry:** SOA typically involves registry protocols as well as discovery, where service providers can register their services and be discovered by service consumers. Each service description is an asset that is configured and leveraged in complete iBPM solutions. Increasingly the trend is to have a unified iBPM repository that organizes the iBPM assets (that in addition to the services also contains various types of business rules, decisions, case structure, flows, and UI.) The iBPM repository can be organized in "layers" along a number of dimensions such as type of product or service, geographical location, and type of customer. The underlying iBPM engine can then invoke a service, apply a rule, or provide a user interaction based on the context of the task or service invocation. This contextual and layered organization and execution of policies and procedures provides tremendous advantages for sharing and customizing the iBPM assets.
- **Composite Applications:** SOA supports the composition of services. Larger-grained services can be built through the composition of smaller or finer-grained services. Thus a dynamic case management solution that accesses internal and external services is a composite solution that itself can become a service producer. The ease of composition of service consumers and service producers in the robust business-oriented solutions is a tremendous advantage of SOA through iBPM. For example, an end-to-end supply chain application built as an iBPM solution can access, through services, various supplier and product information from internal systems of records. It can also invoke external supplier and distributer trading partners. As a composite application, it can provide service interfaces (as a service producer) for its customers to check the status of shipments.
- **Enterprise Service Bus:** Perhaps most frequently when an enterprise embarks upon an SOA project, they consider various types of enterprise service buses (ESB). An ESB is a brokering technology in the plumbing infrastructure backbone of an SOA architectural pattern. An ESB will support brokering of transport protocols, message transformation, reliability, security, and connections to back-end systems. When a message is sent by a service requestor, at the requestor's end point the transport mechanism with the ESB gets involved and communicates the message to the internal ESB layers for further processing. There could be several transport mappings and transformations of the message. The key point is that the underlying transport processing of the ESB allows you to have communication transport independence: A requestor can communicate with a provider via its own protocol without worrying about the provider's protocol. The transport processing mechanism within the ESB takes care of the mappings to and from the various standard protocols. SOA provides integration or invocation of services that are either internal within the enterprise, or are external services provided by third parties. So, in this technological perspective, SOA is very much plumbing and IT-focused.

Cultural Perspective of SOE

Now, as noted above, one of the most important perspectives of service-oriented enterprises is cultural. In this perspective, the SOE views itself as a service producer as well as a consumer for various communities. These communities include customers, to which it provides the best customer experience; shareholders are provided with the best value; and employees are enabled with empowerment, as are partners or outsourcers for optimized service chain management. In this cultural perspective, the SOE provides transparency through automated processes. It demonstrates agility by introducing change or new solutions, or responding to customer requests.

Therefore, a SOE has its focus on customers. But the employees, partners, suppliers, and investors are also communities that need to be served. Service orientation is first and foremost a culture and a mindset. It sees every entity as a "customer" that needs to be served in the best way possible. When a service helps a customer readily obtain the latest information about a product, that is service orientation in action. When a customized product or service is produced within budget and on time, this is also service orientation in action. Almost every type of service work that is carried out within or across enterprises involves policies and procedures, executed as business processes. SOEs focus on handling these various types of communities with very purposeful interactions and the overall efficiency of automated processes.

iBPM and SOA

Service-Oriented Enterprises through iBPM

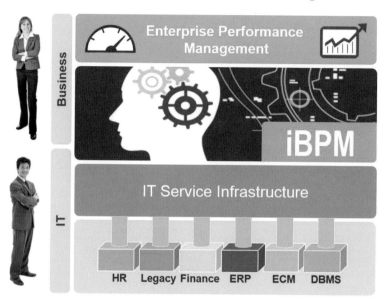

iBPM is the core component that allows organizations to orchestrate their services and provide business (service) value to various communities. As illustrated here, when we look at the service-oriented enterprise architecture, we see at the lower level the IT service infrastructure that provides brokered service access to a plethora of back-end systems or trading partners. These could be the legacy systems, point solutions, or systems of record. At the other end of the spectrum, you have enterprise performance management with business objectives and dashboards.

iBPM bridges the gap between enterprise business objectives and the overall IT services that support them. The road to SOA success runs through iBPM, providing increased business value, the agility to introduce change, as well as automated guidance for human interactions. Human participants, back-end systems, and partner services all become part of the iBPM solution. And yes, this solution leverages the underlying plumbing or infrastructure that is captured in operating systems, networks, multiple service stacks, as well as enterprise service buses.

iBPM delivers the process-level orchestration and integration of services, provided either by internal applications or external trading partners. The iBPM application itself can publish a service. For example, the process flow or an aspect of the application of the iBPM solution can become a service that is itself consumed by other applications. The focus of iBPM is agility and business value for innovation,

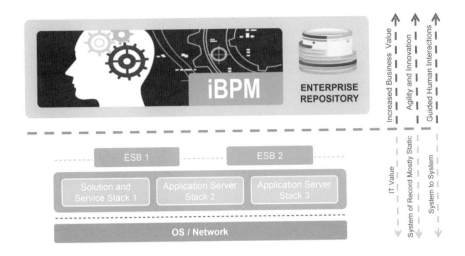

transformation, and change. The focus of the core plumbing and enterprise service bus strategy is on IT value (security, reliability, performance), which is equally essential. iBPM participants include human participant roles as well as services (internal or trading partners). The focus of the service architecture layer through ESBs is on service-to-service integration. The SOA plumbing brokers a standard system integration support that is leveraged by the higher iBPM layer.

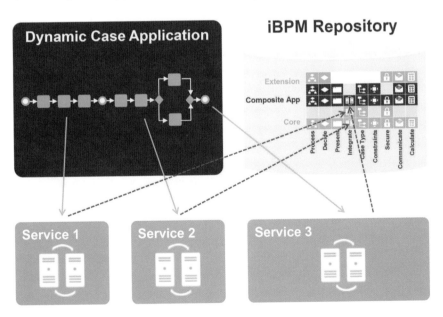

iBPM is both a service consumer as well as a service producer. iBPM can invoke or interact with a service, either directly or through an ESB. Thus, within a process, services are invoked to retrieve information, update, or otherwise invoke a method or operation in a remote service. Similarly, aspects of the iBPM solution could be published as a service. There are two terms that are often associated with business processing involving services—*orchestration* and *choreography*. Please watch how these terms are used as the concepts behind these terms are important, but they are used interchangeably sometimes, and the distinction between these terms is often blurry.

Orchestration deals with the ordering of service execution in process flows. The orchestrated web services are typically executed by a process engine that invokes and controls the services. These ordered services can include trading partners and some of the services can be executed in the context of a transaction. Orchestration of services implies the orchestrated process is actually executed by an underlying process engine.

On the other hand, *choreography* represents abstract processes (in the sense that it is not necessary to have an actual process engine that is executing the choreography), that illustrates the order of message exchanges between applications or more often between trading partners. Multiple parties are involved, and these parties exchange messages of specific types and invoke prescribed operations. So orchestration means there is a process engine that is executing the process, while interacting with or involving internal and external participants. iBPM supports this model. Choreography captures distributed processing involving multiple engines and participants without centralized control (the process engine). In fact, multiple process engines could get involved to realize choreographies.

iBPM Helps Organizations Succeed with SOA

The following five principles illustrate how iBPM can truly become the success enabler for SOA:

1. **iBPM Alignment of Business and IT:** Through an iBPM focus, business and IT can speak the same common iBPM language. iBPM focuses on capturing and automating business requirements or objectives. SOA is often focused on building a strong technical architecture foundation. iBPM helps IT's SOA initiatives prioritize and focus on those aspects of the service architecture that are directly linked to business value. This iBPM focus and prioritization helps link business performance objectives to SOA infrastructure capabilities. It also helps direct the SOA roadmap through business priorities, and not just technical considerations. For example, in a customer service contact center, business and IT can cooperate when building the iBPM solution to improve resolution times. The iBPM solution will leverage the SOA infrastructure, especially in obtaining the most appropriate customer information for the process. This could potentially involve a variety of services accessed via different protocols.

2. **Reuse of iBPM Solutions as Corporate Assets:** The reusable assets in iBPM consist of process flows, UI, different types of business rules, organizational roles, case types, and yes, services. So, services are one of the components in reusable assets that provide business value. iBPM thus provides the business process *context* for reusable services. Services are potentially reused in multiple iBPM solutions. However, for each, there is an iBPM reason and overall context in a business solution.

3. **iBPM ROI Success with Quick Results and a Top-Down Iterative Methodology:** With iBPM, you can start small, achieve success, and grow. More importantly, business stakeholders and IT can quickly realize results with tangible benefits. Sometimes, SOA initiatives are big-bang projects that attempt to completely restructure the technical foundations. The resulting re-engineering efforts take a long time, with little to no tangible results. While re-architecting can be a desirable goal for the long term, it makes it difficult to demonstrate success, especially for the business stakeholders. iBPM can quickly show ROI, while leveraging SOA and infrastructure capabilities. This enhances the visibility and value of SOA.

4. **iBPM Support for Change and Agility:** It is relatively easy to introduce changes to iBPM solutions. iBPM can also organize the changes in repositories that maintain not only services, but also complete iBPM solutions. Typically, changes are realized with zero coding through changing executable forms or models. SOA also claims change and agility. However, agility and change in SOA are considerably more complex. With iBPM, and especially in the business context of change, services can participate in agile solutions. Providing a common "contract," or protocol, SOA initiatives can incrementally improve service implementations while participating in iBPM solutions that change more frequently.

5. **iBPM Intelligence for SOA:** iBPM supports automation involving both human participants and services. In particular, *process* automation includes structured processes, orchestration as well as choreography of services, and dynamic cases. But as we saw in Chapter 4, iBPM also includes a rich collection of business rule types and their execution and analytics for decisioning. The rules and the smart engine that runs them, as well as decisioning based on analytics, can also be leveraged for services. What does that mean? Here are some examples:

   a. **Just-needed and just-in-time invocation of services in a specific context:** This can greatly improve the responsiveness of the dynamic case management solution. Business rules and business logic are leveraged to decide which source to go after, when, and in what connection for a specific interaction.

   b. **Processing and handling of events from services or the application as needed, with business logic applied as needed:** Services are participants. They can have lifetimes and changes of state. They can be late in responding to service invocations. The service responses sometimes need to be correlated to streamline the case processing in the iBPM system.

In summary, iBPM solutions include the active participation of enterprise systems and trading partners. The systems can be databases, ERP applications, legacy applications, document management systems, or any enterprise application required to complete the work. These systems are accessed through service invocations in the SOA which is supporting the discovery, message exchange, and integration between loosely coupled services, using industry standards. Each party complies with agreed upon protocols and carries out its part in the overall execution of processes involving services. iBPM provides the core context for SOA, and bridges the gap between business performance and IT infrastructure, providing an excellent catalyst for SOA success. At the end of the day, SOA needs to demonstrate business value and iBPM needs to fit seamlessly into existing enterprise architectures. iBPM is a great enabler for SOA by aligning business and IT, building reusable assets, showing tangible ROI benefits, and supporting change.

Example: iBPM and SOA in the Public Sector

Vision: A state agency wanted to improve usability of its unemployment insurance benefits system, such as call handling times, training time, and error rates, as well as increase the agility of application development and maintenance. The system was a legacy DBMS environment. Data structure limitations and coding constraints with business logic buried inside the code was burning IT's budget and time.

Solution: At first, the agency made an investment in a software product that helped generate web services from natural code. It then upgraded its mainframe after it overloaded during the economic downturn, but was still not pleased with the performance. Instead of finding another web services product, the agency decided on an iBPM solution. Using a bottom-up approach, it leveraged existing infrastructure to minimize the cost and frustration of further infrastructure development. The iBPM solution provides seamless integration with the agency's legacy DB2 environment.

iBPM generates and consumes web services to considerably increase development agility. Whenever the agency needs to change or update an application, it can wrap the existing legacy system immediately to renew its use and value within the iBPM application. The agency was very pleased to be able to leverage its existing systems. In addition, instead of business logic being hidden in code, iBPM's strong business process modeling capabilities substantially improve transparency for all users, both business and IT.

Results: The agency has experienced increased agility, transparency, and control on the back end, making for easier system maintenance and development. On the front end, the new interface is reducing training time for new employees, enabling users to quickly and easily identify issues with a customer's unemployment claim, and shortening the overall transaction time.

CHAPTER 6

Social Networking and Mobile iBPM

We've looked at how an iBPM fits in the enterprise ecosystem as the core layer between business performance and the underlying technology service infrastructure. But today, enterprises are about *social networking* for greater connectivity, transparency, communication, and collaboration between various internal and external business  communities. Increasingly, organizations are accessing social networking services through mobile devices. This trend is accelerating, and in a few years the majority of Internet access will happen through mobile devices. In this chapter, we cover the relationship between iBPM, social networking, mobile and collaboration.

Social networking is booming via a number of community sites such as Facebook, YouTube, LinkedIn, Google+, and Twitter[20]. Some of these sites have hundreds of millions of members. While the first generation of the Web focused on relatively static websites and a basic Web presence, the current generation of tools and capabilities is a part of Web 2.0. Web 2.0 focuses on interactions and communities, especially social networking, with tools such as wikis, blogs, instant messaging, shared whiteboards, electronic meetings, as well as various types of collaboration portals that allow communities to innovate and share experiences. The other pervasive technology trend is the proliferation of mobile devices (tablets, smartphones)

  as the preferred medium of broadband consumer Internet connections. Mobile technologies have empowered people and accelerated the pace of adoption of social networking. The readiness, availability, and richness of social apps on mobile devices have caused an explosion of social interactions.

The third leg of the stool for this modern and advanced interaction model is the *cloud*. Chapter 13 expands on Cloud iBPM, especially iBPM-driven solutions

---

[20] Facebook is a trademark of Facebook, Inc. Twitter is a registered trademark of Twitter, Inc. YouTube and Google+ are trademarks of Google Inc.

delivered as Platform and Software as a Service (PaaS and SaaS). Most mobile apps and social networking services are actually deployed on the cloud. Mobile cloud computing combines mobile networks to cloud services over the Internet. Thus social networking applications are deployed on mobile devices, interacting with services on the cloud. Since the iBPM solutions can be deployed over the cloud, they can be accessed over the Internet with the appropriate credentials and authorization.

Mobile devices are becoming the preferred option for enterprise solutions and enterprise access. Thus parallel to the explosion of cloud applications, we are witnessing the explosion of "apps" for mobile devices. In fact, the two are coalescing. Solution vendors on the cloud are supporting browser and mobile apps for their applications, with the adoption of the latter far exceeding the former. Similarly, very large enterprises are providing browser and mobile apps to allow their customers access and social interaction.

Collaborating Via Mobile on the Cloud

There are a number of ways that we could classify and categorize social networking via mobile applications on the cloud. Essentially there are two dimensions for this—the *time* of the collaboration and the *place* of the collaboration. The following table lists some of the cloud and mobile enabled tools in the time and place dimensions.

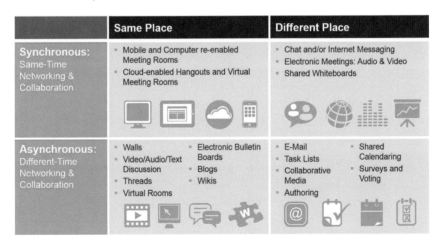

Synchronous collaboration refers to same-time (real-time) communication. This happens when workers are brought together in a single virtual location such as virtual meeting rooms or through telepresence Synchronous collaboration can also take place across locations through the use of chat, instant messaging, webinars, and shared applications. Today, a great deal of work is being conducted throughout the enterprise that leverages synchronous collaboration tools, with webcasts and

instant messaging being the most prevalent. Perhaps the most popular of these is texting (or instant messaging (IM)), which is very trendy among younger generations. Instant messaging and same-time electronic "hangouts" or meetings are other examples of synchronous or real-time/same-time collaboration.

Asynchronous collaboration refers to social networking that is happening at different times. This can be in the same virtual or real location such as a posting on a forum thread or a blog reply. It can also happen in different locations through workflow, calendaring, and traditional e-mail. For example, commenting on YouTube videos, Facebook posts, or on blogs can happen at different times. The most popular of these is e-mail. However, there are also forums and even the ability to create content. Wikipedia would be a prime example of collaboration at different times to create encyclopedic content.

LISTEN to the stakeholders: customers, business managers, employees, peers for a better understanding

COMMUNICATE: through sharing ideas, comments, for improvement

ENERGIZE: through involvement with "fresh" interactions and feedback responses

INNOVATE: through authoring content or building solutions collaboratively

SUCCEED: through involving targeted community members to complete cases or work

Why Social Networking and Collaboration?

Why social networking and collaboration? Well, because social networking and collaboration allow stakeholders, customers, and business managers to be *listened to* and *understood*. Sharing ideas and providing feedback or comments is extremely important. Listening and communicating empowers various stakeholders through involvement in fresh interactions and real-time feedback. They are listened to, and in some cases, they are able to contribute to innovation by authoring content or building solutions collaboratively.

Social networking via Web 2.0 has empowered people with the tools to effectively collaborate in their personal lives. Communities increasingly leverage social media tools such as forums, blogs, social networking sites, podcasts, tweets, RSS feeds, wikis, and others to exchange ideas and interact. Social media has become a powerful channel for customers to provide their commentary on products and services, and organizations are starting to notice the impact of the voice of the network on their bottom line as social media posting can go viral in an instant. One of the textbook examples of this is "United Breaks Guitars",[21] among many others.

Furthermore, social media tools have now penetrated the enterprise to promote intra-communities and exchanges for improvement—this is sometimes called Enterprise 2.0—bringing the capacities of Web 2.0 within the enterprise. Customers, trading partners, and employees are all energized for better communication and innovation through social networking tools deployed on the cloud and accessed via mobile devices. Their voice is communicated and heard in various social communities.

Social networking is also an important channel for the business, especially for social customer relationship management. Increasingly, the communication boundaries between external customers, the enterprise's trading partners, and its employees are blurring with a proliferation of social media tools. This promotes increased transparency and openness, especially for innovation.

For all of these categories, the business needs to have a context for an eventual resolution of the issues raised by the social exchanges. Let's look at how iBPM creates a context of collaboration through *Social iBPM*.

Social iBPM

In the end, it is all about success. In business, entertainment, politics, and almost every facet of life there is a newly re-energized "voice." This voice cannot be constrained within any existing structure or organization. It is a powerful voice that is changing societies throughout the world. And it is a voice that is making and breaking businesses. Reputations rise and fall because of this voice. It is a voice that is leveraged by organizations and individuals alike to create and promote unique

---

[21] A disgruntled customer created a video describing how the airline mishandled and broke his guitar. The posting resulted in 3 million views within one week. See http://en.wikipedia.org/wiki/United_Breaks_Guitars

brands. It is unstoppable and robust. It is the voice of networked communities, often created in an ad-hoc fashion, united through a common interest and made possible through the use of social media.

While the potential impact of social networking is enormous, the real challenge is how to operationalize and realize its potential. All the interactions, tweets, forums, blogs, or wikis will amount to nothing if they are not intelligently mined and translated into action. Through innovation, feedback, and collaboration between community members, the chances of success for specific initiatives or the enterprise as a whole are greatly enhanced. So, what does social networking and collaboration have to do with iBPM? Well, just about everything.

Continuous Improvement with Social

The following illustration shows the continuous improvement lifecycle of iBPM solutions. Starting with directly capturing the business requirements, innovative solutions are built. There are many opportunities to collaborate and network to reflect the needs of the stakeholders during this requirements phase. For example, stakeholders can leverage approval processes, provide feedback on case design, and hold iBPM-enabled sessions to improve the solution.

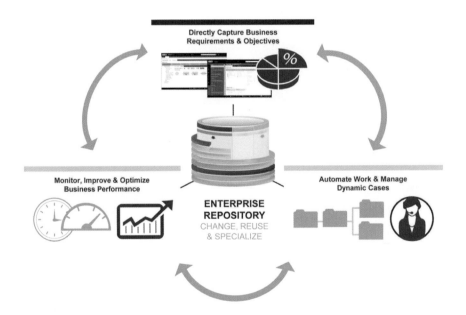

Once the requirements are captured and automated within the iBPM tool, the cases of these solutions and processes are executed. During the execution of the dynamic case, there are ample opportunities for social networking and collaboration, such as discussion threads on the case or live chats with the customer or experts, *all in the context of the moving the case towards its resolution.*

Social networking can also be leveraged in business activity monitoring and reporting drill downs. Business stakeholders can escalate, discuss, provide improvement feedback, and comment on the overall performance of the operators or cases. There is continuous collaborative monitoring and improvement leveraging social networking services. Collaboration in making changes to the assets of the process helps the enterprise, iteratively and continuously, improve the processes as well as the dynamic case management solutions. At the core of this continuous improvement lifecycle, you have the enterprise repository of iBPM assets, such as processes, decision logic, case types, expressions, UI, and integration. Social networking for modeling or process discovery and definition supports innovation by speeding the analysis and definition of processes and case types involving the business.

Mobile and Social for All Phases and All Communities

So, what is the relationship between iBPM and social networking? Well, social networking tools empower and foster innovation in each and every one of the phases of the continuous improvement lifecycle of iBPM solutions. As discussed in the previous section, social networking for modeling or process discovery supports innovation by speeding the analysis and definition of processes and case types involving the business. Collaborative interactions and feedback, whether it is for modeling or for executing the cases, allows the various members of the communities to share ideas, issues, and improvements. Collaboration during the execution of the processes means involving all types of workers—including knowledge workers[22]— and resolving the automated case using the best resources within the enterprise. Social collaboration optimizes and streamlines dynamic case work by the various iBPM participants and parties who form the communities involved in discovering and executing iBPM solutions.

On the other hand, for social networking services, iBPM provides the context of collaboration. In other words, social networking benefits from iBPM. When individuals or communities use various types of social networking tools without iBPM, they are isolated from the business objective or context. It could be as simple as an instant messaging interaction or an electronic meeting. Often, these types of social interactions are isolated and siloed from what is happening with the business processes. The iBPM context answers the questions: Why are we collaborating? At what step in the process? At what phase of the case? For what type of process discovery or innovation?

---

[22] See Chapter 9 for more discussion of knowledge workers.

We can organize the various real-time and asynchronous collaboration opportunities along two perspectives:

- Increased business value
- Increased challenges in collaboration within various iBPM communities.

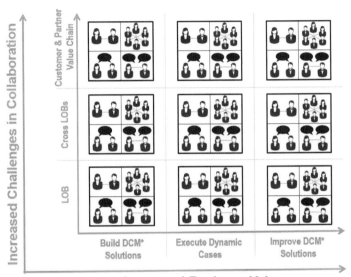

*DCM = Dynamic
Case Management

Increased business value spans the various phases of iBPM solutions including building and discovering process and case applications, executing the dynamic cases, and improving the iBPM solutions. Those are illustrated on the X-axis. On the Y-axis, we have various communities—departments or functional units, lines of business, cross-departmental or business unit functions, and the iBPM value chain. There are at least three categories of societies for social iBPM:

- **iBPM Projects within the Enterprise (Line of Business (LOB) or Cross LOBs):** This is perhaps the most obvious application area for social networking. When building, executing, or analyzing the performance of applications, you can have social interactions between different community members in each phase. The iBPM project can pertain to one business, or span an internal value chain across various functions or lines of business. For instance, a sales process or a customer service process is specific to a functional unit or department. Manufacturing a product, on the other hand, crosses multiple business units such as marketing, engineering, sales, warranty service, and distribution. The fundamental difference is the reporting structure. A process within a function or unit has participants in the process all reporting to the same manager. Processes across functional units or departments imply a matrix organization and are more challenging when it comes to social networking.

- **iBPM across the Trading-Partner Value Chain:** Enterprises typically interact with partners, service providers, suppliers, and customers. The value chain of processes spans across organizations. This is similar across line-of-business processes, but now at a larger, cross-organizational level. As a result, this next level of iBPM collaboration can potentially involve many more participants across a value chain. Here, business-to-business communities can engage in social networking. Expectations and experiences can be shared across organizations. Ideas for innovation can spur the development of new products or services.

- **iBPM Social Communities:** Finally, you have the iBPM social communities at large. These communities can network on iBPM standards, best practices, methodologies, and templates. Sometimes competing organizations become members of the same community. There are several ad-hoc discussions and research communities on iBPM in general, as well as iBPM bloggers. Greater value, however, can be achieved if the community is focused on a particular domain and a particular vertical.

We can leverage real-time collaboration or asynchronous networking tools across the entire spectrum of the iBPM continuous improvement lifecycle. Of course, if we have departmental or functional units, it is much easier to collaborate. The higher we go up on the Y-axis, the more challenging it becomes to collaborate and have social networking with specific value for the iBPM solution.

The potential impact of social networking is enormous. But the biggest challenge is how to operationalize and realize the potential. All the interactions, tweets, forums, blogs, or wikis will amount to nothing if they are not intelligently mined and translated into action. iBPM's continuous improvement phases, including model development, execution, and performance monitoring, can all benefit from social networking . So while social networking supports and augments the various activities of the iBPM continuous improvement lifecycle, iBPM provides the context for collaboration, enabling meaning and relevance for all of the social commentary.

Analytics and Social iBPM

In Chapter 4 we explained the importance and emergence of predictive and adaptive iBPM. Gaining insight from data through data mining and operationalizing the discovered models in the context of iBPM solutions provides tremendous business value. Typically, the analysis of historical data, as well as the use of an adaptive predictive model, applies to structured data which is stored either in transactional databases or data warehouses. Building upon the iBPM/social networking synergy, we can take the potential of social networking to its logical conclusion to determine how businesses can adapt in response to the sentiments in the voice of the network (most importantly their customers) through three critical high-tech advances:

1. Proliferation of social media (discussed above)
2. Dynamic case management (discussed in Chapter 9)
3. Monitoring and analytics, including text (discussed in Chapter 4)

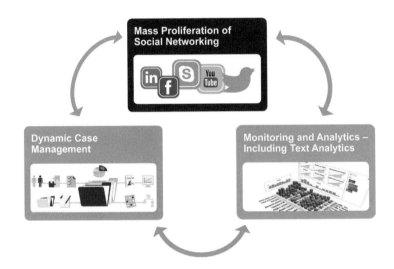

Handling the voice of the network needs all three components in continuous interaction and improvement lifecycles. In the following sections we delve into each one of these and see how they contribute to operationalizing and mobilizing enterprises to respond to the voice of the customer.

As discussed in Chapter 4, predictive analytics is the science behind mining data for repeatable patterns that are reliable enough to serve as a basis for predicting the future. In iBPM, the focus is on the operational execution of the processes and policies that support the business rules. In predictive analytics, the focus is on analyzing the historical data and discovering related patterns or models that incorporate the statistical relationships uncovered in the historical data. iBPM allows you to directly capture and execute the discovered predictive models.

Predictive analytics can be used with most social media interactions, which are text based. When text analytics are applied to the voice of the network, they can evaluate the text included in communications, create analytical models and interpret the intent of the sender. There is a spectrum of techniques for analyzing text including simple filtering, syntactic analysis, and natural language parsing as well as more advanced techniques for recognizing semantics and even sentiment recognition.

Proactively, a company might monitor social media channels and analyze through filters that recognize tokens within text for specific categories, such as product names, company names, dates and times, and location, to name a few. The channel of the text could be social media which is public or posted via e-mails or forums hosted by the organization. Syntactical recognition of specific token types is relatively simple, but can yield interesting results. Combinations of recognized tokens or patterns could be used to create clusters over time, to analyze trends mined from social media. For instance, negative comments about a product brand in a specific region might be indicative of a quality problem in a shipment. Recognizing this in real time and responding to it by halting shipment could potentially avoid embarrassment, bad social press, or worse. iBPM provides not only the analytical capabilities themselves, but also the vehicle by which those analytics connect the voice of the customer to the most impactful actions and business results, especially through dynamic case management. Analytics, by mining the voice of the customer expressed via social networks, help iBPM solutions to not just do things the right way, but do the right thing using dynamic case management, which we will examine in detail in Chapter 9.

How about Mobile iBPM?

So far the discussion has focused primarily on social iBPM. However, in conjunction with cloud computing, the majority of social networking interactions are now conducted over mobile devices. These devices are permeating not only consumer markets, but also the enterprise as the means to conduct business.

An important trend here is the emergence of the *mobile workforce*. Leveraging smartphones and tablets, workers in many industries are carrying out work leveraging mobile applications. Mobile iBPM will allow organizations to seamlessly initiate and complete automated case work via mobile devices. This work will pertain to dynamic cases involving various categories of participants, all interacting via mobile devices. This ability to interact via mobile devices is particularly important given the changes in the mobility of the workforce itself. The instant

accessibility of case status, case work, and case collaboration via mobile means empowerment of a whole new category of mobile workers. Not only are they looking to simply stay connected, they are actually completing transactions and work via smart mobile devices. More specifically, through mobile iBPM workers will be able to:

- View their cases and the work assigned to them
- Monitor the status of cases and workflows via mobile devices to determine potential bottlenecks
- Instantiate new cases on the spot with their mobile devices
- View the details of the case and potentially have social interactions/discussions, comments, notes, etc.
- Carry out tasks on cases, such as approving, rejecting and escalating a case
- Getting events and alerts pertaining to their cases via the mobile device's notification facilities, such as calls, beeps, and voice alerts
- Leverage the mobile device's native capabilities, including rich media, GPS, and camera, to name a few, to complete, augment, and process work

The mobile iBPM capabilities bring substantial productivity improvements to mobile workers. In addition, the consumer now expects a mobile customer experience from their vendors. Thus mobile iBPM applications are needed for both mobile workers and consumers. The latter could use a mobile iBPM application to open an account, submit a claim, or monitor the status of a case. Increasingly, the competitive standard is established by popular apps, such as the ones from E*TRADE® and Amazon®, and consumers expect to have similar experiences with iBPM applications provided by the enterprise.

More importantly, the experience of the worker or the consumer should be consistent across multiple channels including the Web, mobile, or social. One important aspect of the "i" (intelligence) in the iBPM platform is to render the user experience optimally on any platform or device. The iBPM developer should be able to design the graphical interface just once, and then have that interface rendered optimally on each channel, especially smartphones and tablets, by leveraging built-in responsive web design[23] (RWD) features. With traditional development, the user interface needs to be manually tailored for each platform. Given the fact that each mobile operating system has its own specific and different development platform and language, such as Objective C for iPhone® and iPad®, manually customizing the user interface of iBPM dynamic case solutions will be time consuming, error prone and difficult to maintain. Thus "design once and run everywhere" is ideal for agility, speed of development, and support for multiple platforms—as well as maintenance. As the illustration shows, the "everywhere" not only includes smartphones and tablets, but also spans to social networking platforms such as Facebook® as well as the more conventional internal back-office, front-office, and websites of the organization.

[23] Wikipedia (2013). "Responsive Web Design." Last Modified July 26, 2013. http://en.wikipedia.org/wiki/Responsive_web_design

Example: Mobile iBPM Payments

Vision: A mobile payment software company provides an affordable payment platform for mobile network operators, financial institutions, retailers, and brands. Individuals and companies pay businesses on their mobile devices easily, efficiently, and securely. The company wanted the ability to specialize its services that span across different channels, networks, regulatory boundaries, and geographies. It also wanted to reduce time-to-market to keep up with rapid technological advances and cultural trends. Most importantly, the company wanted to capitalize on the massive volume of data collected from consumer's mobile devices to glean valuable business intelligence.

Solution: The mobile platform company chose to address these opportunities through the powerful analytics and decisioning capabilities of iBPM. iBPM provided the company with control and governance of its core platform with the ability to drive customer specialization and flexibility into any area of the world, on any channel. Predictive and adaptive analytics mine the unstructured mass of mobile and social data to create actionable predictive models. The iBPM system presents to customers the next best offer or service on their mobile devices. As the customer relationship grows, iBPM continues to learn more about the customer, enabling it to contextually bring the next best offer or service directly to the individual customer.

Results: The mobile platform company has acquired deeper marketing insights, resulting in enormous financial returns. It has reduced the cost of operations, increased access to new markets, and delivered more services throughout the world.

CHAPTER 7

Legacy Modernization through iBPM

iBPM leverages social networking tools and mobile solutions to support collaboration between various internal and external business communities and provides the context of collaboration. But even as enterprises take advantage of these modern tools, the reality is that there are still many incumbent enterprise resource planning (ERP), point solutions, and home-grown legacy systems (most often in archaic programming languages such as COBOL), that are difficult to understand, maintain, or change. Putting "lipstick on the legacy pig" does not work. These systems are typically systems of record and are essential for "keeping the lights on." However, they are difficult to maintain and do not inspire agility. In this chapter, we focus on legacy modernization through iBPM.

There are many reasons why organizations need to modernize. The following highlights the pain-points associated with legacy systems:

- **IT Overwhelmed with Maintenance–Not Innovation:** Often, organizations have millions of lines of undocumented code. In some organizations, upwards of 80% of the IT budget is spent maintaining legacy code or legacy systems. This is the main reason why IT has a project backlog and cannot keep up with the demands of the business.
- **Legacy and Retiring Workforce:** Some legacy systems are home-grown programs written by increasingly aging and retiring programmers. This disappearing workforce keeps the policies and the procedures, as well as how to work with these legacy systems, in their heads. Since the code is typically undocumented, there is a real danger of losing the reasoning and business logic embedded in the code.
- **Ossified Processes and Business Logic:** ERP or point solutions are closed systems. The business processes and business logic are both hidden and difficult to change or customize. With these type of solutions, there is an initial honeymoon period, where the solution seems to fulfill business requirements. However, very soon the need for customization and specialization becomes apparent, and the ERP and point solutions prove difficult to extend and customize.

- **Sophisticated Decisioning:** Within legacy and ERP systems, it is difficult to automate and handle sophisticated business decisioning and business rules. A separate mechanism is required to extend and specialize these systems to capture the business rules and sophisticated decisions.
- **Manual Intervention to Handle Exceptions:** In advanced organizations, exceptions are the rule. Exceptions could be raised by the ERP or legacy systems, or they could go unnoticed with dire consequences. Exceptions need to involve knowledge workers to handle complex decisions. For instance, assessment of potential fraudulent transactions, approvals for large financial transactions or processing of applications that have unconventional cases will involve workers who are knowledgeable about the policies and procedures with exceptions.

For many organizations, the number one challenge is changing or upgrading existing applications and legacy systems. Implementing or customizing new applications, and making changes or adapting are the other two top priorities within organizations. To address these challenges, organizations embark upon legacy modernization initiatives. Unfortunately, these initiatives often fail.

Why Do Legacy Modernization Initiatives Fail?

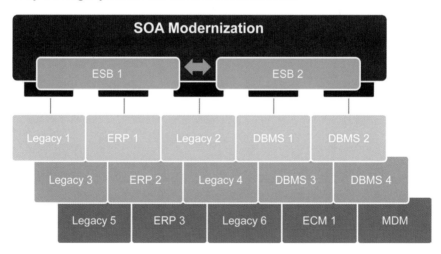

There are four main reasons why legacy modernization efforts fail:

1. **Big Bang Modernization Initiatives:** Often with the best intentions, huge and expensive initiatives are launched with modern architecture paradigms, especially with service-oriented architectures (SOA). Since there are so many legacy systems and the attention is on infrastructure and plumbing, these "modernization" projects under the banner of SOA waste many cycles and resources with little or no business value.

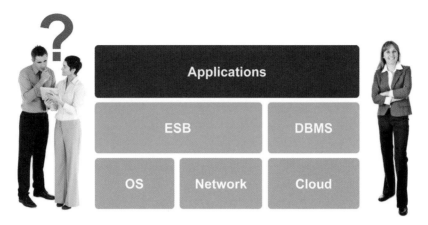

Big- bang SOA projects typically deploy one or more enterprise service buses and attempt to expose, as services, a large number of legacy, ERP, or database management systems with no clear business objectives. ESBs can be overkill—a solution in search of a problem. A lot of effort is spent on architectural integrity in the forms of paper-ware and model-ware, with little or no immediate benefits. In other words, the modernization project is just a bottom-up approach focused almost entirely on modern SOA plumbing.

SOA patterns have their place and are often essential. But overhauling large collections of applications with a SOA stack from the bottom up, layer by layer, with no top-down justification or rationale is the wrong approach. As we have discussed, a modernization initiative needs to "Think big, but start small", introducing incremental business value. Large rip-and-replace monolithic initiatives cannot keep up with iteratively changing market opportunities, customer interests, business drivers, government mandates, and compliance requirements. There needs to be a clear roadmap of inexpensive incremental modernization steps that balance business visibility and ease of implementation.

2. Equating Modernization to Modern Languages, IDEs, Components, and Platforms: Another reason why modernization initiatives fail is that they often equate modernization to adopting modern languages or modern component architectures, frameworks, or methodologies. These tend to be very complex and require many artifacts, or they embed a lot of the business logic in code that is cryptic for the business.

Large organizations often have millions of lines of legacy code written in older languages such as PL/I, COBOL or C. There are also many examples of code written in proprietary languages such as SAP ABAP™. Some modernization initiatives have attempted to replace or extend/expand legacy code with more modern coding using languages such as Java, C#, or JavaScript. These languages and companion component frameworks are hip. The problem is that object-oriented or component coding is still coding! The business logic is still embedded in the code and it is cryptic to the business, providing little or no business transparency. These supposedly modern programming languages do have advantages as they provide a lot of flexibility and improve productivity by going from structured languages to object-oriented languages, tools, components or frameworks. The problem is that they provide value *for IT*. IT resources often love these languages and platforms and reject modernization through iBPM at inception. But these languages do not enable business-centric modernization, aligning business with IT. When is the last time you saw a business stakeholder go through Java code or use Eclipse?[24]

3.   **Ignoring the Human Participants in Modernization Initiatives:** Legacy modernization also involves cultural change and needs to include human participants in the modernization initiatives, as they are impacted the most. Often, human participants and cultural impacts are ignored in favor of technology. As the previous point illustrated, modernization is usually equated with IT modernization in the overall enterprise architecture stack while ignoring the human participation. Actually, legacy systems, ERP systems, home-grown systems and even modernized versions of these typically elevate exceptions to humans. Managing exceptions can be the majority of the effort in an end-to-end process, and these are thrown to humans with no governance, automation, or enablement. If you take the total effort involved in resolving a customer service request, just focusing on the operational or system areas without looking at the automation or enablement of the human experts who must handle exceptions results in partial and incomplete modernization.

Then again, how about the standard processing of tasks (vs. the exceptions)? Well, here you have the flip side of the human dimension—the resistance to change. Since employees are trained on familiar (legacy) systems, replacing them without understanding how the modern solution will make their lives easier results in an inherent resistance to change. In addition, approaching modernization with the same data-centric mindset that still requires business users to be dependent on desktop procedures, knowledge management, and training to use multiple siloed systems will not yield the most business value from the initiative. This could jeopardize the success of the project, so ignoring the human participant will put the modernization initiative at great risk.

4.   **Ignoring Governance and Center of Excellence for Modernization:** At the end of the day, no initiative can succeed without oversight and governance. This is an obvious statement, but often a core cause of failed modernization initiatives. By now, it should be obvious that modernization initiatives are complex. They involve many legacy systems, home-grown solutions, legacy extensions, undocumented

---

[24]   http://www.eclipse.org/

code, and a maintenance nightmare. That is the 'fait accompli' side.

Then you have the stakeholders: IT with a desire for modern architectures and languages; a diverse user community, some of whom are dissatisfied with the current status and others who are wary of new solutions and change in general; and perhaps most importantly, business managers and executives frustrated with cost overruns, delayed projects, and systems that cannot keep up with business objectives. The larger the initiative (the big bang), the more difficult its governance. If a modernization project takes too long, by the time it is finished, it no longer meets the needs of the business stakeholder. Modernization needs a Center of Excellence (COE) with specific governance involving best practices, prioritization, and project monitoring as discussed in Chapter 3. Modernization projects will have much less of a chance for success without an established COE that oversees the people enablement, the processes for best practices, and the prioritization of modernization projects.

How does iBPM Help Legacy Modernization?

So far we have identified the problems and challenges of legacy modernization using traditional approaches. Then how does an organization succeed in legacy modernization? There are four robust ways where organizations can achieve concrete modernization results through iBPM, addressing all the challenges and issues:

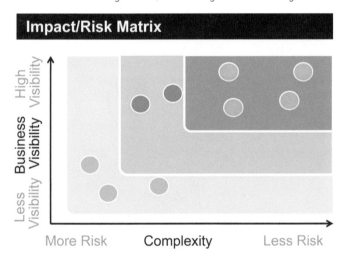

1. Think Big, Start Small with iBPM: It is difficult to find big-bang, long duration and expensive IT modernization projects that have delivered on their promises. Bottom-up IT and technically focused re-architecting simply does not work. The iBPM approach is top-down *and* incremental, from business objectives to operationalized iBPM solutions. While the overall "big thinking" transformation and modernization vision will drive the initiative, iBPM lets you start small with projects that can easily demonstrate business value, while minimizing risks.

In any mid-sized or large enterprise, there will be many potential projects for modernization and transformation. Analyzing quantitatively the projects that will provide business value and reduce risk will help prioritize the transformation roadmap and quickly demonstrate value from low-hanging fruit. On the impact/risk matrix, there is less and less complexity, which means less and less risk as you go right on the X-axis. As you go higher up on the Y-axis, you have higher and higher business value and visibility. Each of the bubbles in the diagram illustrates a specific iBPM-focused project that could be used to modernize a legacy system or application. These are called "slivers," which are essential to success. After the initial successes with iBPM solutions modernizing legacy deployment, the roadmap and maturity towards complete modernization can proceed in incremental and iterative phases, always demonstrating value and concrete results along the way. In addition, as the requirements for modernization and solutions change, iBPM can keep pace with these changes, ensuring success—and no one will argue with success.

2. **Equate Modernization to iBPM:** A business is defined through its policies and procedures. In building iBPM applications you are actually constructing an enterprise repository (assets) of these policies and procedures. These include business rules of different categories as well as your process flows. The repository also includes your information models (data), the user interaction (UI), and integration (services). Modernization means to directly model and automate the business and procedures in iBPM solutions. The business rules, process flows, and cases become explicit and visible so that the business and IT can collaborate to change and evolve them.

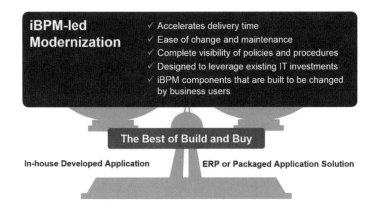

Modernization should be viewed holistically. On one end of the spectrum, legacy and ERP systems can be "wrapped" through iBPM solutions. Wrapping means that business solutions, including end-user operators and customers, interact through an iBPM solution, which in turn accesses legacy services as needed. In some cases, the legacy solution is retired or replaced. At the other end of the spectrum, you have the constant need to customize, improve, and respond to change requests. With traditional approaches, this is attempted through in-house development and IT-driven coding. iBPM-driven modernization brings the perfect balance between these two. With iBPM, the business and IT can speak the same language, communicated through modeled and automated policies and procedures. The transparency and visibility of the processes provide a unique opportunity to continuously change and enhance the business solutions. So iBPM becomes the foundation for modernization with distinct advantages—accelerated development and deployment of business solutions; complete visibility of policies and procedures; ease of change and maintenance. All this, while leveraging current IT investments and modernizing the enterprise incrementally.

3. Automate Processes with Human Participants—Transactional, Knowledge-Assisted, and Knowledge Workers: As we have discussed, legacy systems often raise exceptions that need be handled by human experts. This creates silos between the legacy solutions and manual exception case processing. iBPM aggregates these through wrapping legacy systems as noted above, while at the same involving the human participants needed to handle exceptions with complete visibility. We will expand on the different categories and types of human participants in Chapter 9. Suffice it to say here that the cognitive knowledge workers who are essential for managing complex exceptions, can now become active participants in dynamic case management solutions automated through iBPM.

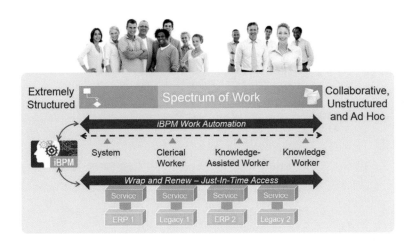

This automation of human activities and collaboration for all types of work (structured and unstructured) as well as workers, especially in the context of legacy systems, is an important milestone in information technologies. The vast majority of processes within organizations are either simply documented with no automation, or ad-hoc involving a plethora of tools. Modernization with iBPM automates, augments, assists and guides human workers in all categories. iBPM targets the modeling and execution of processes that can handle both the simple, straight-forward path as well as exception cases involving legacy systems and humans. The human participants can be assigned tasks and controlled by the iBPM solution so that business users have end-to-end visibility and service level governance. It is the governed, automated, guided, and collaborative execution of processes involving human roles or skills as well as back-end legacy systems that make iBPM solutions extremely effective in modernizing and transforming businesses holistically.

4. Implement iBPM Centers of Excellence and Governance: As discussed in Chapter 3, no initiative can succeed without oversight and governance, and a COE is the best route to achieve these goals. In terms of legacy modernization, COE governance needs to reflect iBPM processes, people/roles, standards, decision making, and deliverables that target modernization. Ideally, this governance is complemented by an iBPM platform that provides tools and constructs to help you directly realize the objectives, guidelines, and governance practices of the iBPM methodology. In each iteration and phase of the methodology, you would like to have the corresponding function in the platform that helps and guides you in realizing the objectives of the iteration or the phase.

Modernization Best Practices & Methodology 	iBPM Business Architecture	Customer Staff Enablement & Self-Sufficiency
▪ Wrap and Renew Best Practices ▪ Design & Implementation of Service Interfaces ▪ Testing Best Practices ▪ Project Methodology ▪ Project Intake Process	▪ Deployment Strategies ▪ Modernized Application Architecture Blueprint ▪ Modernization Reference Architecture ▪ Common Infrastructure for Legacy/ERP systems	▪ Training & Certification ▪ Mentoring & Guidance ▪ Lessons Learned ▪ Workshop Advanced Design Topics ▪ Hand off & Transition

◄──────────────── **iBPM Governance** ────────────────►

For modernization, iBPM COE governance should specify:

•   Modernization Best Practices: The adoption of best practices, methodologies, and guardrails to guide team constituents is a core mission of the iBPM COE. Given the fact that iBPM is the best bet to incrementally modernize and transform iteratively, while responding to continuous change requests, an agile methodology is essential. The best practices specify how end-to-end modernization and wrap-and-renew dynamic cases should be implemented and operationalized, with the system-of-record static parts delegated to ERP or legacy systems while the differentiated and innovative cases, subcases, and processes are managed in iBPM. The iterative COE methodology identifies the participants, artifacts, and phases of iBPM projects. iBPM agile methodology is covered in more details in Chapter 10.

- **Modern Business Architecture:** iBPM is the core of the modern business architecture, as we will see in Chapter 11. The COE governance rationalizes the application repertoire of the enterprise, determining the applications that need to be built as iBPM solutions; the incumbent applications that need to be wrapped; and those that need to be deprecated. The governance also specifies the end-to-end reference architecture—from business strategies to iBPM solutions to the underlying IT infrastructure—required for legacy modernization. Often, modernization is equated with SOA initiatives, and, as we saw in Chapter 5, the best way to achieve SOA success is through iBPM. For service interfaces to legacy systems, the iBPM COE is also responsible for the creation and management of reusable legacy integration assets.
- **Enablement:** Because iBPM is a paradigm shift in building and deploying applications, the COE needs to provide the promotion, training, and certification of iBPM development talent within the enterprise. For modernization, the iBPM COE governs the best architectural modernization design patterns and continuous improvement strategies. iBPM is not a panacea, and even with the best iBPM approach, governance and continuous monitoring of results are essential to success.

The Journey to Application Rationalization through iBPM

Enterprises are living organizations. They grow; they acquire and merge; they extend and expand. Responding to business pressures, organizations often do not have the time or focus to govern the growth of their application inventory across the globe. Invariably, there will be duplicate applications, unnecessary applications that sit on the shelf, and legacy applications that have run their course and must be retired.

As organizations grow rapidly, demands to respond to market pressures often force them to act before thinking or analyzing the growth of their business application needs. The term "shadow IT"[25] refers to business stakeholders acquiring applications directly from (often cloud) vendors without involving the formal IT channels. With the emergence of cloud-based applications, it is not uncommon to find business owners, who control the budgets, acquiring applications without consulting the IT organization (or doing so after the fact.)

---

[25] http://en.wikipedia.org/wiki/Shadow_IT

All applications are not equal. Some applications need to be retired. Others are mission critical, but the customization and maintenance of these can become prohibitive and time-consuming for IT. Analyzing quantitatively, while balancing risk and business value, will help prioritize the transformational road map and quickly demonstrate the value of low-hanging fruits. In large and global organizations, each line of business will have its own portfolio of applications. One danger is to conduct a paralysis-through-analysis exercise to gather the inventory of all the applications. While eventually all applications need to be rationalized, a better approach is to quickly identify the most business impactful applications and modernize these first, expanding the iBPM-driven application modernization inventory over time.

For legacy modernization and transformation through iBPM, there are multiple dimensions to consider in rationalizing applications and, of paramount importance, rationalizing the inventory to identify the best candidates for modernization. To develop a rationalization inventory and prioritize and select projects for iBPM application modernization, consider the following quantitative and qualitative measures:

- Business Value: How important is the new or modernization candidate application to the business stakeholders? Some of the generic measures are increased revenue, controlling or decreasing cost, regulatory compliance requirements, risk mitigation, and access or security constraints.
  In a centralized model, where all decisions are channeled through a core central IT, there will be conflicts as different line-of-business stakeholders will have conflicting priorities. Federated agile teams, coupled with corporate governance and a center of competency approach have proven a far better methodology for iBPM modernization.
- Variability Measure: How frequently will the business logic, business decisions, business policies, and business procedures change? How frequently are they changing in existing deployments? As discussed above, there is a sharp contrast between systems of record that do not change much and agile innovation, transformation, and agility systems that change much more rapidly.
- Maintainability Measure: How expensive is it to maintain the current legacy application or custom code? There are many reasons why maintaining an existing application could be costly or prohibitive. Old, undocumented code for important applications can become a liability. For packaged applications, another consideration is the existence or health of the independent software vendor and their commitment to upgrade or maintain the application. There are also legacy people who have the knowledge of the application in their heads. Once these people have left the company or retired, the knowledge is gone.
- Complexity Measure: For wrapping opportunities, how much effort will it be to integrate with the legacy systems? Integrating with an old

system or application that does not have a robust and modern application programming interface could be problematic. There are also other considerations such as the operating system or platform, language and age of the application. Transactional consistency, the number and frequency of interactions, and the overall persistent database structure are other considerations in the complexity dimensions.

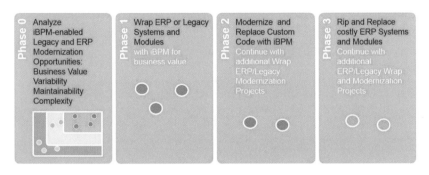

Once the candidates that represent the low-hanging fruit or slivers for modernization are identified, the journey to modernization through iBPM can proceed as follows:

Phase 0: Modernization Roadmap and Inventory: In this phase, it is important to identify the quick-win slivers, taking into consideration the dimensions discussed above—business value, variability, maintainability, and complexity measures.
Phase 1: Phase 0 will yield several candidate projects for modernization and transformation. These candidates are likely to be projects that wrap existing legacy or ERP applications. This phase starts showing ROI and true business value through automating work and cases, while integrating with and leveraging current incumbent solutions.
Phase 2: This phase starts to tackle modernization projects by replacing custom code, either in proprietary (e.g. ERP vendor-specific languages) or standard languages. The custom code attempts to address limitations in the ERP or packaged solutions.
Phase 3: The last phase is the retirement-and-replacement phase, where legacy systems that are no longer viable or too expensive to maintain are deprecated and replaced with iBPM solutions.

The Value of Modernization with iBPM

As we have seen, successful iBPM automation starts with those projects that have the least amount of risk and the highest visibility for the business. In fact, iBPM becomes the incremental agility layer for wrapping legacy applications while leveraging existing systems as needed. iBPM is always driven by business objectives and provides a holistic perspective on modernization, involving human participants, human roles, human skills, and organizational structures.

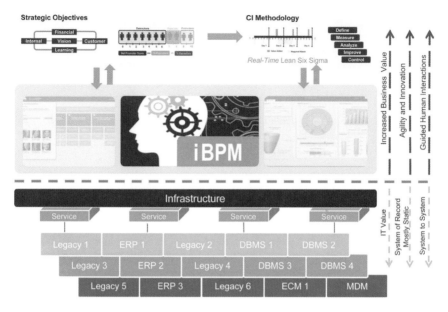

With the ability to modernize in incremental phases, you can easily change policies, procedures, flows, dynamic cases, different types of business rules, decisioning rules, constraints, expressions, and event rules. iBPM uses these policies and procedures to automate work, while providing multi-channel interactions to internal operators or customer-facing websites and mobile devices. It provides a context for social networking and collaboration, and allows organizations to engage in end–to-end dynamic, unstructured, and collaborative cases. iBPM supports activity monitoring, analytics, business rules, and decision management and provides the best mechanism for successful SOA initiatives. It's clear that the way to succeed with your modernization efforts is through iBPM.

Example: Modernizing for the Future

Vision: A financial group's credit card business has grown its portfolio of accounts by 50% over the past two years and plans to continue aggressive growth in both domestic and international markets. Management was convinced that service excellence was the key to success in this highly commoditized business, but the group's credit card service operation was not positioned to grow with the business. Day-to-day service fulfillment activities were inefficient and complicated by the underlying system infrastructure. Legacy systems were expensive to maintain, and functionality needed to support new card products could not be developed on those inflexible solutions. The group's client service operation was organized into many specialized support and fulfillment teams, structured around cumbersome systems and manual processes required to fulfill customer requests. Delivering excellent service at the point-of-interaction via 'one-call' resolution was rare as existing processes did not let agents resolve most customer issues at first contact. In the back-office, mundane administrative tasks (such as the re-keying of data into various systems, organizing and shuffling paper documents, etc.) delayed resolution. The time spent on value-added activities such as case review and selling was limited as skilled analysts were consumed by administrative tasks.

Execution: The financial group decided to address their legacy infrastructure issues with a complete system overhaul. iBPM was selected as the technology to provide a full servicing solution, "wrapping" around a new core processing platform and automating processing activity from the call center through to the back office. Key benefits of the new system would include a 30% increase in one-touch customer service resolution and a 70% reduction in average resolution times for requests and requiring back-office intervention. The deployment would deliver both an improvement in service excellence as well as cost savings through streamlined operations.

Results: iBPM provides a 1080, high definition solution to optimize the customer experience and automate operations for call center staff in Toronto, London, Montreal, and India. Full account and transaction information is provided on the customer service representative's desktop. Intent-led service processes enables higher levels of customer service and 'one-touch' issue resolution. Process automation capabilities are able to process basic requests straight-through. Issues that cannot be resolved directly at the call center are automatically routed to central workbaskets used by all back-office dispute and fraud staff. Smart routing capabilities assign cases to staff from the centralized workbaskets. Paper-based processing and manual re-keying of data have been eliminated as electronic case data is routed to the appropriate personnel automatically.

50% of the back office dispute staff was redeployed, and a 95% reduction in IT compliance cost was realized.

CHAPTER 8

Real-Time Lean Six Sigma

So far, we have focused on the role of iBPM in the enterprise ecosystem. In Chapter 1, we discussed how the adaptive enterprise evolved from a number of continuous improvement methodologies, especially Lean Six Sigma, and how iBPM can be a powerful approach for optimizing business applications. In this chapter, we will focus on how enterprises can achieve Lean efficiency and Six Sigma effectiveness through iBPM. Through iBPM- enabled process improvement, enterprises can keep processes under control, remove waste, and achieve all the Lean/Six Sigma objectives in real time.

Real-Time Lean

What is Lean? Lean focuses on increasing process efficiency and reducing waste. There are three types of work:

- Work that is unnecessary waste as it does not add any value and must be eliminated.
- Value work where the real work gets done.
- Work that is required waste, such as regulatory or legal compliance. It is not *the work*, but nevertheless must be done.

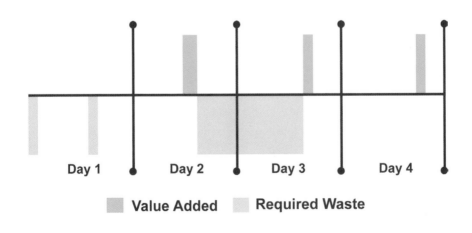

There are two critical measures in Lean: *lead time* and *process efficiency*[26]. Lead time is defined as:

$$\text{Lead Time} = \frac{\text{Amount of Work in Process}}{\text{Average Completion Rate}}$$

In Lean, the objective is to reduce the lead time. This could be achieved by either decreasing the numerator (amount of work in process), or increasing the denominator (speed of process completion).

The other measure, process efficiency is defined as:

$$\text{Process Efficiency} = \frac{\text{Value Add Work}}{\text{Lead Time}}$$

Process efficiency reflects the percentage of actual work being done. Often, in the end-to-end execution of processes, there is non-value work, such as wasted efforts switching between green screens, copying and re-copying customer information (and propagating errors), replication of effort across the enterprise, waiting for downstream processing, and so forth.

The objectives of reducing lead time and increasing process efficiency could be achieved if as much waste is eliminated as possible and the work is done at a greater speed. Let's look at an example that happens every day across the globe. In a back-office environment, an employee might be going from one office to another, collecting signatures and shuffling documents. Walking, traveling, or taking the elevator between office floors does not add value to the work. It is waste. As another example, in the front-office, a customer service representative might be toggling between various screens, copying the same information pertaining to a customer from one screen to another. This too is waste. An example of required waste (though the members of the discipline might disagree!) is legal work undertaken to ensure compliance to internal or external regulations. The *value work* is what really matters, especially from an internal or external customer perspective. Therefore, in Lean, the objective is to increase the percentage of value work in the end-to-end processes.

Without a complete iBPM solution automating policies and procedures, a majority of the work is waste. In fact, with iBPM, most of the waste is eliminated and a lot of the required waste is reduced. Even the value work is improved through automated, guided interactions.

---

[26] See Michael L. George (2003) *Lean Six Sigma for Service.*

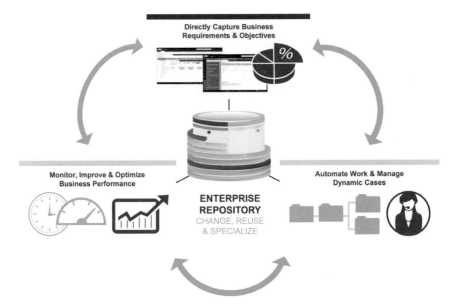

iBPM eliminates waste and improves process efficiency throughout the lifecycle of business solutions with unique capabilities including:

- Directly capturing business requirement.
- Automating the work in dynamic cases, with straight-through processing and guided user interactions.
- Continuously monitoring and improving business performance, with complete visibility and transparency.
- At the core of the iBPM continuous improvement lifecycle, there is the enterprise repository of reusable assets including process flows, different types of business rules such as decisioning rules, constraints, expressions, event rules, as well as integration and user interfaces.

Let's look at each of these capabilities in detail.

Operationalizing Business Mandates through Directly Capturing Requirements: Reducing waste and effort from the point of defining requirements to actual process automation are very important characteristics of iBPM that directly tie to Lean. In traditional approaches, for instance, there is a lot of waste when importing, exporting, and translating between different types of artifacts, from business mandates all the way to coding. Typically, many different tools are used—word processing for documents, business analysis tools, enterprise architecture tools, design tools, and coding tools, to name a few. There is a lot of waste in translating between the various representations of these tools and keeping them synchronized. As explained in Chapter 2, with a unified iBPM solution, the waste and overhead of going from requirement specifications to analysis, to design, to coding, and so on, is completely eliminated, bringing tremendous benefits to the business stakeholders. Furthermore, the waste of translations from imports, exports, and overall inefficiencies in building business solutions is eliminated.

Other Technologies: Multiple Tools – Export/Import

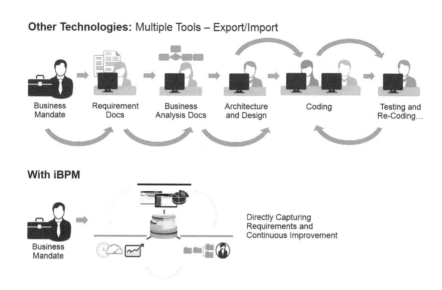

With iBPM

Directly Capturing Requirements and Continuous Improvement

Automating Case Work: Another area which is extremely important for Lean is work automation and dynamic case management to eliminate manual work. In the

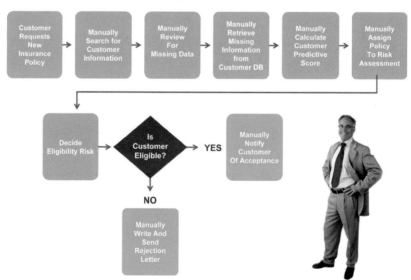

before-and-after illustration from Chapter 2, we can see there are many wasted and error prone tasks: manual searches, manual data entry, and manual application of policies. This is the as-is state that incurs unnecessary work processing and is typically slowing the completion of tasks.

In addition to automating the *processes* in a case hierarchy, iBPM leverages business rules and decisioning automation to streamline the as-is state. There are four process optimizations that improve the lead time of processes when automated through iBPM:

- Automation of the tasks
- Automation via straight-through processing (obtaining the right just-in-time information)

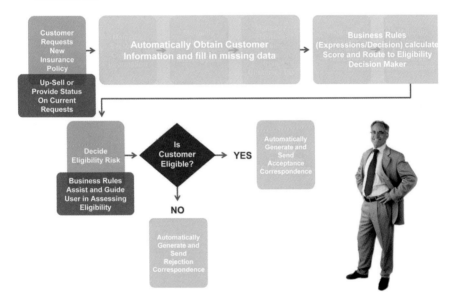

- Leveraging business rules for automating policies (e.g. eligibility and risk)
- Intent-driven and guided interactions to get work done faster

Each of these contribute to improving process efficiency, enabling a higher percentage of value-add work and substantially reducing lead times. For tasks that require human participants, iBPM provides guided and purposeful interactions. Sometimes, manual tasks can be completely eliminated through rules and straight-through processing. The decisioning, the availability of the resource, and the skills of the resource are taken into consideration to eliminate waste.

With iBPM, the tasks are automated in the context of *dynamic cases*. As we shall see in Chapter 9, a case is the organization, coordination, and dynamic collaboration of multiple tasks for a business objective. Cases must be dynamic as new tasks can be added dynamically, and cases may also need to respond to and generate events. With dynamic case management, knowledge workers can also collaborate and participate in the resolution of cases, especially those involving complex exceptions and knowledge work. This means time does not have to be wasted by unnecessarily involving subject matter experts, and the speed of resolving cases is accelerated.

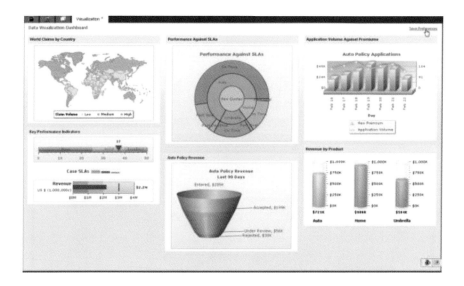

Business Activity Monitoring: As cases are executing, rather than chasing various types of databases, spreadsheets, e-mails, and other forms of communication to determine a measure of the performance for the cases, iBPM provides business activity monitoring (BAM) capabilities. All the waste incurred in chasing data and information for performance measurement is eliminated because iBPM keeps track of the various activities and presents them to the business users in meaningful, actionable—and real-time—reports.

Enterprise Repository for Reuse and Specialization: The traditional approach of copying or replicating assets between multiple applications is wasteful and inefficient. At its core, iBPM provides a dynamic, multi-dimensional enterprise repository which keeps track of all the assets, specializes them, and organizes them across many dimensions. This means that new processes, new rules, or new cases are easily added. With iBPM, various types of applications with contextual, situational information are all maintained in the enterprise repository. This provides tremendous benefits to process efficiency and realizes the potential of real-time Lean as the enterprise repository optimizes reuse and supports specialization to eliminate waste when building new applications or evolving existing ones.

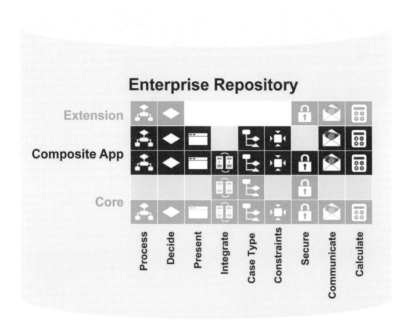

Enterprise Repository

Real-Time Six Sigma

Six Sigma
Improve Quality and Reduce Variation

Lean looks internally at front-, mid-, or back-office processes and attempts to get rid of the waste and improve efficiency. How about Six Sigma? As mentioned, Six Sigma is a complimentary methodology which focuses outside-in on the voice of the customer. Lean focuses on reducing waste and improving process efficiency. Six

Sigma attempts to improve quality and reduce variation. In fact, Six Sigma has a very specific statistically quantitative objective, where the process is kept under control for its critical-to-quality measure (CTQ). This measure should not exceed upper or lower limits—the *control* of the process. The CTQ is a specific business measure that defines the objective of the Six Sigma initiative. It could be a measure of unit, time, dollar amount, or just about anything that is measurable and associated with the process being improved. The quantification for keeping the processes under control is keeping them within plus or minus three standard deviations, 99.9996% of the time. There are many methodologies that are associated with Six Sigma. The most popular of these is DMAIC: Define, Measure, Analyze, Improve, and Control.

Traditional Six Sigma projects tend to be very long in duration, big bang, and complex. Each of the phases and steps in DMAIC or other Six Sigma methodologies has many deliverables. The "M"–measure–is perhaps the most challenging phase as the data can have quality issues, the sources of the data are many and dispersed, and the aggregation of the data is difficult, to name a few.

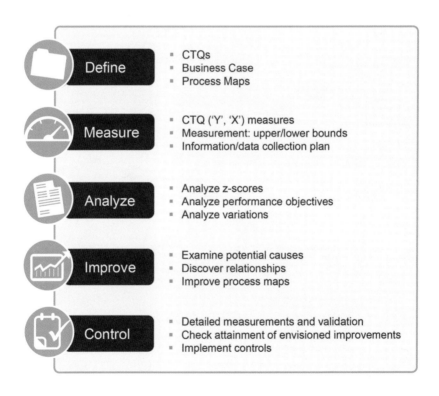

With Six Sigma, the objectives of improving quality and reducing variation could be achieved if the CTQ measures are mapped onto properties, or states of the cases or processes that are automated in the iBPM solution. This enables the iBPM solution to watch and make sure the processes are under control. iBPM can potentially escalate or take proactive steps when process CTQs exceed or fall below the upper and lower limits. These define the control perimeters of the process. The iBPM system keeps processes under control, in real time. Contrast this to traditional Six Sigma, where data needs to be collected, analyzed, and then the processes need to be fixed after the fact.

A CTQ (also identified as big 'Y') can also depend upon other properties (big 'X's) all managed by iBPM cases. So, all the phases in the continuous improvement lifecycle of iBPM come into play to achieve the objectives of Six Sigma methodologies, such as DMAIC, in real time. In fact, many organizations achieve the objectives of Six Sigma without going through all of the detailed steps and phases of DMAIC or other Six Sigma methodologies. This does not mean that the rigor of these Six Sigma methodologies must be abandoned. It does mean, however, that the best and fastest way to achieve Six Sigma objectives is to introduce iBPM in all phases of the Six Sigma (and Lean) methodology.

The CTQ or big 'Y' measure itself could depend on other measures that contribute to its value (big 'X's, small 'y's and small 'x's). These correspond to the internal capabilities that contribute to the overall CTQ of the end-to-end process. For example the CTQ could correspond to overall Net Promoter Score improvement with a specific reduction in detractors or improvement in promoters or both. Once captured and represented as a measure (Y), it can depend upon several layers or values that influence it:

- The call center hold time, which itself needs to be controlled, such as not exceeding the prescribed amount of 30 seconds, 99.99996% of the time
- The quality of the next best offer and its acceptance rate
- The on-line banking access time
- The branch waiting time

The point is that each of these measures (the small 'y's) contribute to the overall objective (the CTQ or big 'Y') and need to be in control. In traditional Six Sigma improvement, there are many complex phases, and the process is improved most often after the fact by measuring and analyzing the historical data, often from multiple sources.

When the process is executed using iBPM, the big 'Y's as well as big 'X's, small 'y's and small 'x's are all identified as properties of automated cases and processes. The relationships between these measures are captured in declarative expressions, business rules and constructs of iBPM. This allows the process improvement experts to directly capture and represent expressions and relationships between variables/properties (e.g., a big 'Y' is a function of a big 'X'). Similarly, small 'y's (big 'X's) can be expressed in terms of small 'x's. More importantly, since iBPM provides an automation and execution environment, the iBPM's engine can monitor these values and readily take action or escalate if any of the measures exceed their prescribed upper or lower limits, or are in danger of doing so. For instance, if the time it takes to process a call or a claim starts to get into the "red" zone (service level violation), iBPM can execute temporal event rules to immediately alarm and notify the case worker or her/his manager. It can even automatically execute event handling rules to keep the process in control.

Therefore the benefits of *real-time* Six Sigma (i.e. Six Sigma process improvement through iBPM automation) can be summarized as follows:

- **Holistic Modeling and Automation:** iBPM allows users to model and deploy Six Sigma processes holistically and cohesively, including properties, process flows, cases that potentially span multiple teams, decision rules, expressions, event rules, service levels, system integration, and user interfaces.
- **Directly Capturing CTQs: Y, X, y, x:** Process improvement experts can have properties depend on other properties through several levels of dependency, which provides a framework for managing multiple levels of 'x's and 'y's. The calculation and propagation of property values is automatic. Several types of decision rules are used to support the business logic that keeps the processes in control. Analytics—predictive or adaptive—can also be leveraged for the overall optimization of the processes, providing for instance the Next-Best-Action for the customer, and improving the CTQ measures that influence the customer's Net Promoter Score.
- **Real-Time Monitoring and Response:** Multiple types of event rules, including constraint violation, temporal events (such as service levels), changes in the state of cases, and so forth can trigger easily specified actions to keep the processes in control and make sure CTQ boundaries are not violated. Constraint rules and conditions can be used to monitor performance against upper and lower specification limits and take appropriate action when limits are exceeded. Service level rules allow users to specify various temporal limits, such as goal and deadline, and take appropriate action when a limit is exceeded. If property values that represent 'y's fall outside prescribed boundaries (called *Lower Specification Limits and Upper Specific Limits*[27]), the iBPM application can automatically act on those exceptions with the appropriate response.
- **Ease of Specialization:** As new processes and situations are discovered in the Six Sigma analysis, the project team can easily modify and specialize existing processes, rules, and other elements of the iBPM application. As noted earlier, by leveraging the dynamic multi-dimensional repository of the process assets, the intelligent iBPM engine can apply the right constraint for the CTQ measures depending upon the circumstance, for instance treating different customers

---

[27] Wikipedia (2013). "Six Sigma." Last Modified August 28, 2013. http://en.wikipedia.org/wiki/Six_Sigma

differently, depending upon their level (silver, gold, platinum), their history, the geographical location and the type of service or interaction. All these can be taken into consideration to apply the most specific, customized, and specialized constraints for a particular situation.

Real-Time Lean Six Sigma

iBPM allows process improvement projects to achieve *real-time efficiencies (Real-Time Lean) through real-time effectiveness (voice of the customer – Real-Time Six Sigma).* Now, there is a robust relationship between Lean and Six Sigma. It has been shown, practically and analytically, that the more we get rid of non-value (or waste) work, the faster we can achieve the Six Sigma objectives. This makes sense intuitively, and the analytical data backs it up. In other words, as we get rid of the waste in processes and improve their efficiency, we will be able to achieve the objectives of Six Sigma (CTQ process measures within specification limits 99.9996% of the time), much faster. With iBPM, process improvement projects can focus on value chains to reduce and eliminate waste in all the phases of the agile, iterative, and continuous improvement lifecycle of iBPM projects. As waste is eliminated, the process reduces variance and improves its quality. In other words, through iBPM Lean accelerates reaching Six Sigma objectives and keeping the process CTQs in control.

Example: Lean Six Sigma and Global Contract Manufacturing

Vision: A global contract manufacturing provider faced the task of producing a wide assortment of products for its distinctively unique global customer base. It provides manufacturing in different domains such as defense, aerospace, life sciences, with tens of plants globally. The supply chain for each customer is different and requires certain guidelines and processes to be followed. Demand volatility for the manufacturing services provider was also a challenge. Customer orders rarely went unchanged, and any changes to orders caused waste. Operating at such a large and unpredictable capacity, the company needed to identify problems in real time. Work cases typically travel through a series of hierarchical escalations before they are resolved. These escalations needed to happen faster and more efficiently.

 Solution: The manufacturing provider adopted a Lean deployment strategy. Its strategy was the centerpiece of its operating system portal which is where work gets done. The iBPM-developed portal easily enables knowledge workers to initiate, progress, and share case work. iBPM gathers process metrics automatically, which can then be visually analyzed through business activity monitoring capabilities. These reports allow the manufacturing provider to identify where there is waste and eliminate it, all in real time. From there, best practice processes are continuously replicated across the company. Smart automation eliminates unnecessary manual steps to hasten escalations so that case work is completed faster.

Results: The global contract manufacturing provider realized several hundreds of millions in savings due to its Lean strategies. It is reaching its Lean and Six Sigma strategy objectives faster and has given the customer a voice. Productivity has grown significantly with hundreds of thousands of work cases closed annually. Lastly, as the contract global manufacturing provider continues to rapidly grow, it can scale its strategy and continue to monitor and respond to change through iBPM and their Lean/Six Sigma methodologies.

CHAPTER 9

Dynamic Case Management

This chapter focuses on a very important capability within iBPM: The ability to manage processes and collaborative tasks holistically to realize business objectives—called *dynamic case management*. Here are some of the pain points with which business stakeholders struggle:

- How can our many applications work together?
- How can we be more flexible? Why do changes take such a long time?
- Why is it so difficult for me to have complete end-to-end visibility into my operations?
- Why do processes have to be so structured? Why can't I do unplanned work?
- How can we easily innovate and collaborate about new ideas?
- How can we easily coordinate multiple work streams, content, workers, and solutions?
- Why do we have so much manual processing that is slow and are error prone?
- Why am I not able to have a case across my business units?

Why Do Organizations Need Dynamic Case Management?

Dynamic case management addresses the questions above and much more. In real-life business applications, what is being executed are actually "cases," not individual or siloed process flows. The value proposition of dynamic case management can be summarized as follows:

- **Dynamic yet Organized Automation:** Usually a case involving multiple workers, multiple departments, multiple applications and content is *partially* automated. Some work streams will be done via e-mails, others via departmental workflows, others managed via spreadsheets, and still others via green screen legacy solutions. With dynamic case management, you can have one solution that automates and coordinates all the tasks. The organization of the tasks involves subcases, each of which targets a specific objective contributing to the overall business goal of the case.

- **Holistic and Cross-Departmental:** Another very important advantage of dynamic case management is to support end-to-end holistic processes involving many departments. In an overall value and supply chain, each department and team can focus on a subcase contributing to the overall objective of the parent case. Modeling and executing this with the rigidity of flowcharts and swim lanes will be very difficult.

- **Social and Collaborative:** All the social iBPM advantages that were discussed in Chapter 6 can be leveraged in the context of dynamic cases. Case workers and managers can leverage discussion streams, synchronous exchanges or chats, knowledge wikis, opinion blogs, targeted tweets—all within the context of the dynamic case and its objectives. Thus with this (somewhat ad-hoc and flexible) social collaboration, the case stays alive and continuously improves with innovative idea exchanges.

- **Agility and Flexibility:** A very important reason why organizations need dynamic case management automation is *flexibility* to manage improvements for reduced cost, reduced risk, and increased efficiencies. This agility means some tasks are planned and others are unplanned. Workers and managers can dynamically add ad-hoc tasks and even discover the need for new processes in the context of an individual case. This flexibility also includes supporting variations in work, smarter work processing, and social collaboration to achieve business objectives.

- **Handling Exceptions and Design-by-Doing:** Exceptions happen. In traditional iBPM approaches, the exceptions are handled outside the scope of the solution, and via different streams such as e-mails, meetings, ad-hoc exchanges, etc. As noted above, the agility and flexibility of dynamic case management allows exceptions to be handled in the context of a case—naturally and seamlessly. Furthermore, as ad-hoc and unplanned tasks, as well as subcases or process fragments are added to a single case, they can be used to update or create a new case template so that subsequent cases can benefit from the way the exception was handled. Workers take action (e.g. add ad-hoc tasks), and then these are used as the basis of improved design, which is design-by-doing.[28]

- **Engaging Knowledge Workers:**[29] These are the cognitive workers, the subject matter experts and often the authors of policies and procedures. Traditionally they are siloed and do not engage in operational processes. That is changing with dynamic case management, and this very important category of workers is becoming increasingly more engaged in operationalized cases, especially with the seamless integration of social networking and collaborative capabilities within the case.

- **Empowering Knowledge-Assisted Workers with Guided and Intent-Driven Interactions:** An even more important category of workers who are supported through dynamic case management are the knowledge-assisted workers.[30] This

---

[28] Creating case templates from best practice case instances.

[29] For more details on knowledge workers see: Davenport, Thomas H. (2005). *Thinking for a Living*. Boston, MA: Harvard Business School Press.

[30] For more details see: http://pega.com/community/pega-blog/knowledge-assisted-workers

most common category of worker leverages the decisioning, business rules, and situational/contextual execution of interactions in particular to help them complete their specific, contextual work within the case hierarchy.

What is a Case?

A case is the coordination and collaboration of multiple parties or participants that process different tasks for a specific business objective. The coordination of the tasks is organized in a case hierarchy (subcases). Cases will always have a subject which is often a human such as a customer, patient, or recipient of welfare. A case, however, can be almost anything, such as a claim. The case will also have a business objective pertaining to the case subject. There will be a lot of collaboration between various case workers to resolve the case. While processing these tasks, a case will have content, often from multiple enterprise information systems or content management repositories.

Some of the tasks will be planned in predetermined process flows, and some tasks will be unplanned. All of these coordinating tasks in the case are for a concrete business objective or goal. Cases are therefore dynamic, adding or changing any of their elements, and responding to and generating events.

In fact, if we were to look at the anatomy of a typical case, as illustrated here, the case will have a hierarchy. It will have subcases, and various tasks will be executed in the context of the parent case or one of its subcases.

Cases generate and respond to business events. Sometimes, events need to be correlated. Workers can subscribe to events and be notified on the occurrence of simple or complex correlated events. Cases will have service levels. There will be different types of policies and business rules, such as decisioning rules, expressions, decision tables, and constraints, which are associated with the case. Cases have multiple process fragments executing in the context of the case hierarchy.

Cases will go through milestones or "stages." Business will have complete visibility into these milestones and can easily monitor the progression of the case's lifecycle towards resolution.

Structured Flow versus Dynamic Case

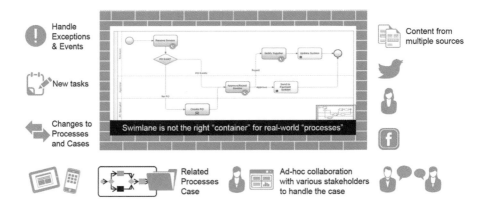

If we look at traditional iBPM, it tends to be structured and the process steps tend to be predetermined. The swim lane is perhaps the most ubiquitous representation of traditional production processes, where each of the lanes indicates a participant or a party. The most important aspect is that the sequencing of the tasks is rigid and predetermined. The swimlane is not the right "container" for real world processes. These involve social collaboration, related cases, and ad-hoc tasks. It boxes in and limits what could be done with process automation. It is a partial "fragment" of end-to-end dynamic and collaborative real-life processes. The exciting tasks, events, collaboration and other work streams happen outside the limitations of the flow chart, or traditional BPM implementation.

Dynamic case management can handle these structured processes, but can also handle robust hierarchies of tasks and collaborative processes with ad-hoc changes. In the following illustration, you see the folder paradigm depicting the case. It has business objectives, subjects, and case workers. It also involves various business rules or policies, as well as process fragments. You can also see a number of enterprise information or content management repositories providing content or data to the case. As the case progresses, there could be additional subcases, process fragments, tasks, sources of information, or content that becomes associated with the dynamic case. The key point is that adding policies, procedures, content, structure, and responding to events could all be done dynamically.

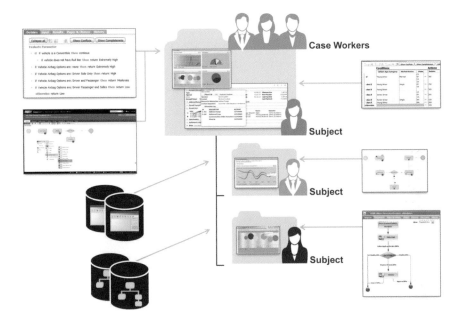

As noted, when we think about iBPM, we sometimes visualize the swim lane representation of a process. There are events in the process map, and the ubiquitous diamond shape represents decision branching. This is what some people think of when you say "business process management." The problem is that tasks and their sequencing are predetermined ahead of time. When designing the process, you need to have thought about all of the branches you have, all the tasks, events, sequencing, and so on, which is pretty much an impossible task. In real life, one needs to be able to handle structured predetermined processes, as well as unstructured and collaborative ad-hoc tasks within dynamic cases.

Let's look at an example of dynamic case management where you might be executing one of these swim lane process diagrams. You initially start with a business objective, a case subject, case workers, and a number of document management or ERP systems that are feeding data to the case. There are business rules or policies that are driving the case towards completion. Then, dynamically, and without any prediction ahead of time, you might create a subcase with a different subject. You might execute a different unstructured process fragment. You might have several of these changes with additional accesses to enterprise content, repositories or other enterprise systems, as well as execute additional tasks. The point is that, yes, you are executing tasks in the context of process flow fragments, but there is an additional dimension of holistic, collaborative, and ad-hoc work. You are able to handle exceptions, include other tasks, and manage dynamic events, all in the context of the aggregate case.

Dynamic Case Management with Knowledge Workers

The two dimensions illustrated here, representing the type of case worker and the spectrum of work from structured to dynamic case, capture the scope of case management. The spectrum of workers begins with clerical or manufacturing workers. In this domain, you know exactly what needs to be done and every task can be predefined and predetermined because workers in this domain tend to have well-defined, structured work. At the other end of the spectrum is the knowledge worker. Knowledge workers are the experts. They are cognitive workers. They innovate and often come up with the policies and procedures in the organization. They can react on the spot, knowing what to do in a particular, exceptional situation. Between these two, you have the most important category that represents the majority of workers, the knowledge-assisted workers. The knowledge-assisted worker falls somewhere between the clerical worker and knowledge worker. Knowledge-assisted workers need to apply policies and procedures in the work that they are trying to complete. They are not creating the rules, but they must apply the rules, often situationally or contextually. Customer service representatives are a good example of knowledge-assisted workers. They are usually trained so that when they interact with a customer, they know what to do within the context of the specific situation.

In addition to these types of workers, there is also a spectrum of *work* in dynamic cases. The spectrum spans short duration production workflow to dynamic cases. ("Collaborative," "adaptive," and "unstructured" are other adjectives often associated with this more flexible type of work processing.) Dynamic cases tend to be longer in duration and more collaborative than structured, predetermined workflows. You want to automate this type of collaborative work to provide guidance to the knowledge and knowledge-assisted workers. You want to be able to dynamically discover processes, modify policies, change the hierarchy in the case, add or change tasks in the case, and add or modify content or any other aspect of the case. You want to be notified and respond to business events. You want to have a holistic view of the tasks originated in hierarchies. You want to support collaboration, as well as the coordination of the tasks to meet a business objective. So, dynamic case management becomes critical, especially for knowledge workers and knowledge-assisted workers.[31]

The key point is that iBPM is able to handle the entire spectrum of structured, semi-structured, as well as unstructured case processing that sometimes tends to be longer in duration. The lines between these types of work are actually blurry. iBPM solutions supporting dynamic case management are able to support the case spectrum and more importantly, move from one to the other very easily. You might, for instance, start with a traditional production workflow and end up with a much more collaborative and unstructured case.

Dynamic Context

One important aspect of dynamic case applications is the context of the case. The dynamic enterprise repository contains the core iBPM assets. What are these assets? These are the case types, process fragments, integration with various back-end enterprise content management or legacy systems, as well as the different business rules such as decision trees, decision tables, analytics, expressions, constraints, event rules, and also the various forms of Web and mobile interactions. These assets are needed in business applications to process dynamic cases. The assets are organized along multiple dimensions that represent the business intent, such as the type of product or service you are offering, the level of the customer (e.g. Gold, Silver, Bronze), and the jurisdiction or location of the interaction. The specific values for these dimensions constitute the context of the case.

Depending on the type of the product or service, type of customer, or location of the case, the underlying iBPMS engine picks the most appropriate process fragment, data source, business rule, or form for the case worker or the case subject if you have a self-service interaction. Instead of worrying about what discount to provide

---

[31] It should be noted that knowledge workers and knowledge-assisted workers also use structured work in, for instance, their procurement applications or different types of HR applications.

a customer at a specific level, the iBPMS application picks the discount rule and executes it automatically. In other words, the case is aware of the context of that particular interaction and executes the appropriate iBPM asset accordingly.

Dynamic Case Lifecycle

Cases have a lifecycle. When a case gets created, it is opened and different types of case workers, such as knowledge workers, knowledge-assisted workers, and clerical workers process the case. Often they work on various tasks in parallel. There could be ad-hoc changes, such as creating subcases, adding tasks, running additional unstructured processes, or adding content.

At some point, the case is resolved. Ideally, you would like to complete the case and say that the case is closed. Sometimes, a new case is rejected or is recognized as a duplicate. In any of these situations, the case is considered resolved. In some situations, the case needs to be reopened, taking it back to the "open case state." When the case is reopened, all of the documents, the case data, and the status of various tasks and processes are all available to the reopened case.

Dynamic Case Management for all Industries

 **Financial Services**

- Credit card dispute case
- Account opening case
- Customer servicing
- Customer on-boarding

Healthcare

- Care/disease management
- Rehabilitation services
- Healthcare claim
- Behavioral health treatments

Government

- Welfare
- Tax audit
- Citizen service case
- Grants

 **Insurance**

- Claims: auto
- Claims: disability
- Claims: medical & life

 **Manufacturing**

- Supply chains
- Warranty claims
- Services
- Innovation

As we have discussed, dynamic case management supports all types of case workers and case processing. There are many industries that deal with cases, whether it is credit card disputes in card services, exceptions handling and fraud investigations in corporate banking, customer service requests in retailing, disease management in healthcare, welfare management in the government, or claims management in insurance. All of the characteristics that we have mentioned earlier for handling structured and unstructured cases or the ability to add tasks dynamically, manifest themselves in these types of industry applications.

Let's look at a specific example of a case for automobile warranty claims processing. In this example, there are two business objectives for the dynamic case management solution to manage warranty claims:

- Increase the number of satisfied customers by increasing promoters (following Net Promoter Score methodology) by 20%.
- Reduce overall claims processing by 30%.

As illustrated, the subject of the case is the Claim. The super-case is the Auto case. It has three sub-cases: Tire Damage, Oil Change, and Anti-lock Braking System Fault. There are tasks executing for the objectives and completion of each of these subcases. For instance, returning parts is a task that is part of the Repair Fault sub-case within the ABS Fault sub-case. Each of the sub-cases will execute one or more process fragments. Tasks are assigned within processes. So there will be a process flow for verifying parts return, and tasks such as Pay Dealer are executed at a specific step within that flow (process fragment).

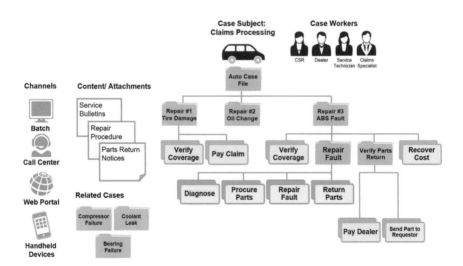

Sometimes tasks are not predetermined or planned. In the context of a particular sub-case, the case worker might need an ad-hoc or unplanned task. Both planned tasks that are associated with a step in a process fragment and unplanned tasks are supported in dynamic cases.

Dynamic case management is an important feature of iBPM. As illustrated here, what drives the case and its sub-cases to completion are the various business rules, decisioning, event rules, integration and guided user interactions which make up the intelligent neurons and the nervous system of the case.

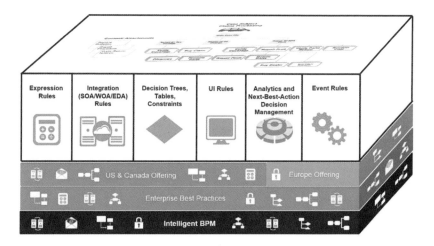

Note that since this is an iBPM approach, all these capabilities—business rules engine, analytics for decisioning, event correlation, etc.—are part of the unified platform. Rules and decisioning control and drive the case to completion.

Example: Taking Off with Dynamic Case Management

Vision: An air transport company that operates one of the busiest airports in the United Kingdom wanted to deliver a refined service to its 65 million annual travelers. As complicated as airport operations are, the 75,000 employees divided into air, tower, and ground teams are dedicated to providing an easy and comfortable flying experience for their customers. To do this, the air transport company wanted to increase its overall operational efficiency, have a consistent view of flight status across all stakeholders, and grow collaborative decision making among its employees.

Solution: The air transport organization used iBPM as a backbone for its European Airport-Collaborative Decision Management initiative. iBPM enhances the decision making process by seamlessly integrating with existing operating systems and automatically acting on data in real time. Within the system, each aircraft turnaround is handled as a case, and in order for case work to be completed, the system drives collaboration between a number of human participants (such as flight crew managers, refueling and cleaning crews) and systems (such as air traffic control). iBPM automates key airport processes using rules specialized to each circumstance. For example, the system schedules departures and arrivals to minimize the time each aircraft spends on the ground, stationary or taxiing. In response to abnormal scenarios, such as weather delays or a terrorism alert, it downloads the rules sets that the company has designed to manage the new situation and invokes a new resource plan. It intelligently routes work and data to the right knowledge worker.

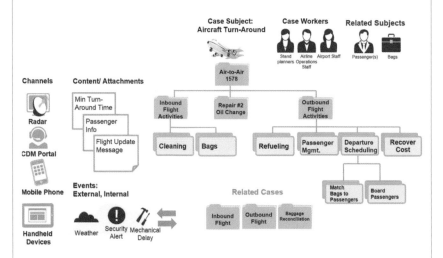

Results: The implementation of iBPM raised the on-time departure rate from 68% to 85%. The air transport company operates at a 98% runway capacity so that more flights with more happy passengers can take off more frequently on time. Due to the operational efficiency, the company pays fewer penalties, has reduced its environmental impact, and schedules and uses expensive resources more accurately while providing a safe, comfortable flying experience for all of its customers.

CHAPTER 10

iBPM Agile Methodology

The fact of the matter is that an iBPM is great raw material. To make it successful, you need a complimentary development methodology. In Chapter 3, we focused on success factors for iBPM. We mentioned specifically iBPM methodologies and COEs. The previous chapters also elaborated on additional advanced capabilities for iBPM including iBPM and Business Rules as well as Analytics (Chapter 4), iBPM and SOA (Chapter 5), Social and Mobile iBPM (Chapter 6) and Dynamic Case Management (Chapter 9). We also discussed how iBPM can serve as a great enabler for improvement, transformation and modernization of enterprises—Chapter 7 on Legacy Modernization and Chapter 8 on Real-Time Lean Six Sigma.

Agile methodology focuses on the science and art of how to build agile solutions using iBPM. It helps the various roles and participants building the iBPM solution with a precise implementation approach that specifies:

- Phases and iterations
- Roles and responsibilities
- Step-by-step tasks and iterations
- Milestones
- Deliverables of the iterations/phases
- Overall governance from the requirements to the deployment of the iBPM solution.

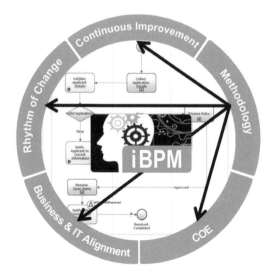

The methodology also provides the blueprint and overall management of the project for the iBPM implementation. As illustrated here, the iBPM methodology is an important and essential cornerstone of the COE, the lingua-franca and dynamics of communication between business and IT, the governance of the change that is always constant, and the continuous optimization and improvement of process solutions. An iBPM project succeeds or fails in relation to the methodology adoption and governance.

Five Principles of iBPM Methodologies

In order to implement a successful methodology, there are five core principals and requirements that must be met including:

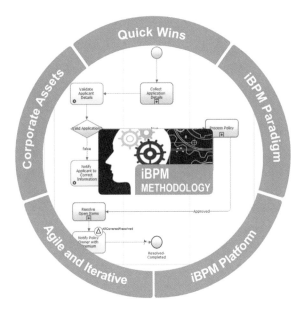

- Realizing quick wins through the methodology
- Understanding the iBPM paradigm for the enterprise
- Grasping how iBPM methodology can leverage the iBPM platform
- Recognizing agility and iterations in the iBPM methodology
- Building corporate iBPM assets through the iBPM methodology

Quick Wins

The methodology starts with the business case and identifies a best-choice opportunity (quick win or low-hanging fruit). The earliest phases of the methodology need to identify a business case and then define the best-choice (what to implement first) opportunity to guarantee the success of the iBPM deployment.

There are several factors that make up the business case. Higher level motivations include:

- **Innovation:** Ability to create and quickly introduce new products and services. Innovation can also impact new approaches for existing processes.
- **Growth:** Related to innovation is a focus on growing revenue as well as the market share of the business.
- **Cost Control:** With the economic downturn of recent years, organizations are increasingly looking for solutions to control cost and "do more with less."
- **Productivity:** As enterprises attempt to control costs and grow, the directive to increase employee productivity becomes essential. Productivity also spans customers, trading partners, and other serviced communities.
- **Compliance:** A substantial percentage of IT and business resources are spent dealing with compliance issues.

Careful analysis and quantitative and qualitative ROI are critical in this initial business case phase. Once a business opportunity is identified, there are often many use cases that could potentially be digitized and automated. The iBPM project leader needs to decide where to start and which of the candidate use cases should be deployed first. This choice is critical for the overall success of iBPM projects. If the wrong decision is made early on, a project may run longer and cost much more than the initial estimates. Identifying and agreeing upon which use case to automate first is an important success factor that business and IT need to agree upon in the initial phases of the iBPM project. One proven approach is to choose a quantitative strategy that attempts to discover the use case with the least effort and highest business value.

We have seen this illustration in Chapter 7 on legacy modernization. As you go to the right on the x-axis, you have less risk and less complexity. As you go up the y-axis, you have higher and higher business value and visibility. Each of the circles represents a potential iBPM project for automation. We should re-emphasize our "Think big, but start small" strategy here with a focus on the quick win to really demonstrate the value proposition of iBPM. Mostly likely, your best choices for a quick win are the projects in the upper right corner, such as account opening in our example here. There are other projects for consideration as well, like claims processing, though the business visibility is slightly less and the risk somewhat higher. Another potential project is the time-off request which has the least amount of risk because it is a relatively simple application, but does not provide great business value or visibility. The quick-win opportunities could be identified through:

- Brainstorming sessions with stakeholders
- Quick-win calculator
- Automated iBPM quick-win project selector, and
- A combination of these methods

The New iBPM Paradigm

iBPM is a new paradigm and a new way of thinking about solutions deployed across the extended enterprise. There are principles that are common with any good software development lifecycle (SLDC) and agile methodologies such as Scrum.[32] These approaches have phases, workflows, "sprints," roles, and artifacts that are adjustable and applicable to iBPM. In iBPM, you are trying to elevate the programming paradigm so that processes and business rules are captured, represented, and implemented directly. Furthermore, the main drivers in iBPM are participants that have new and emerging roles such as business analysts and process architects.

Business & Business Analyst

Business and IT Collaboration in iBPM Methodology

IT & Process Architect

---

[32] https://www.scrum.org/

Capturing and implementing change in iBPM iteratively is quite different from waterfall conventional programming methodologies which typically:

1. Complete a detailed requirement/functional specification phase, then
2. Complete the design phase, then
3. Spend an inordinate amount of time building it, and then
4. Deploy it, potentially conducting acceptance testing, towards the end.

Typically what happens in Step 4 is that the business stakeholders can quickly introduce additional changes or indicate what has been built is not what they asked for or wanted.

With iBPM, you have continuous communication with the stakeholders and can incrementally test and deploy an iBPM solution in collaboration with those business stakeholders. Furthermore, ideally the business stakeholders are *part* of the team building the solution. As we have discussed, this is possible because iBPM provides constructs and solutions *that the business understands and can change*. iBPM assets such as processes, different types of business rules and even the UI can be communicated via readily and easily understandable forms that provide a common language between business and IT. In some scenarios, business participants can introduce new process flows or rules directly in the deployed iBPM solutions. These business participant roles are different from the more technically-oriented architect and development roles with different competencies, talents, capabilities and responsibilities that need to be captured and reflected in the methodology. With iBPM agile methodologies, conventional software development walls, roles and challenges are obliterated in favor of *model-driven development*. Modeling can and needs to quickly move onto automation and execution with as little mapping or switching of tools as possible, and with none being the best option.

The iBPM Platform

For a successful iBPM project, an iBPM execution platform is needed. The agile methodology should reflect and leverage the iBPM platform that will be executing the business processes, decisions, and business rules. The iBPM platform supports the iterations as you are building the iBPM solution.

For example, in Scrum you will have a prioritized product backlog—a list of business and technical features that need to be implemented. Each of these is mapped onto iBPM elements, such as business rules for risk, approval cases, integration with bug fixer, etc. Ideally the Scrum team includes members from business, IT, and operations who are proficient in iBPM. With agile iterations in each sprint or even daily Scrum, the stakeholders—especially the business—have direct visibility and access to the solution that is being built. Even the decision when to ship or consider a solution productized can be adjusted. Ideally the iBPM Scrum methodology should use the terminology, roles, portals, and meta-models of the target iBPM platform.

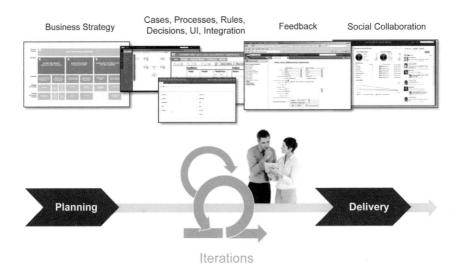

There are other ways in which the iBPM platform and methodology support each other:

- **Best Practice Pre-Flight (Deployment) Analysis:** The iBPM platform can capture best practices as specified in the methodology and conduct a pre-flight analysis to check if the best practices are reflected in the solution that is about to be deployed. This analysis can also identify and warn about potential areas of conflicts or problems, again reflecting the methodology's recommendations.
- **Change Requests Process:** Improvement and change requests are also processes. iBPM can support processes to directly capture and automate incremental change requests, in other words, processes for process improvements. This meshes improvement with development. It allows various stakeholders to readily instantiate improvement and change requests, involving the details of the request in the context of the business application being built.

Agile and Iterative

Agility is paramount. The methodology should help you continuously monitor and measure your improvements, as we discussed in regards to real-time Lean Six Sigma in Chapter 8. Before starting an iBPM sliver project, there needs to be a clear understanding of its purpose or return, which is then continuously measured and monitored once the solution is deployed. Iterations can subsequently address the return objectives, such as the Lean goal of getting rid of additional waste or the Six

Sigma goal of improving quality and reducing variance. In other words, the deployed iBPM solution is continuously measured and improved to achieve the business objectives that drove its implementation. There are three types of iterations in the agile iBPM methodology:

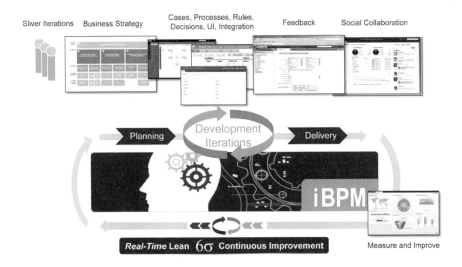

1. First, the slivers which iteratively automate additional products, services or problem domains and solutions. You identify the number of slivers by starting with the low-hanging fruit (the "quick win"), but there are other projects as well in your backlog of iBPM solutions.
2. Second, as described above, you have the iterations of the Scrum methodology: daily Scrum meetings and sprints. This iteration occurs during the construction, design, building and deployment of the iBPM solutions. The essential element here is to quickly demonstrate results through the iterations, and provide immediate visibility to all stakeholders.
3. Third, after deployment there are also post-deployment iterations. These post-deployment iterations and delta improvements ensure that the critical-to-quality measures and processes are in control. The ROI is continuously monitored to ensure the solution is on target. Occasionally, you introduce delta enhancements and corrections which are incremental improvements (small "dot" versions) to the iBPM solution.

Build Reusable and Situational Corporate Assets

iBPM is strategic and ideally should be deployed for enterprise-scale transformations. Organizations should be able to reuse the solutions they are building and easily specialize each solution for different lines of businesses or geographical areas. As we discussed in Chapter 8 and elsewhere, the core of the continuous improvement lifecycle of iBPM is the dynamic repository of the corporate assets. This brings us to our last principle for iBPM methodology, which is that it should encourage you to build assets in a dynamic multi-dimensional repository including process flows, case types, business rules, decision management strategies, business events, service integration and the UI elements for browsers, social networks, and mobile devices.

It is important to be able to organize these corporate assets along a number of dimensions. The methodology needs to help you specialize, extend, or expand them incrementally. For instance, you might have many of your business processes and declarative rules that deal with risk management shared across many iBPM solutions. Risk calculation, risk mitigation, exception handling for risk management can be shared throughout an organization for different purposes. You also should have the flexibility to specialize and apply the most appropriate risk rule for specific situations or circumstances. The methodology should be able to leverage the capabilities of the iBPMS to create these assets in an organized fashion, provide support for reusability and also specialize when needed for situational execution.

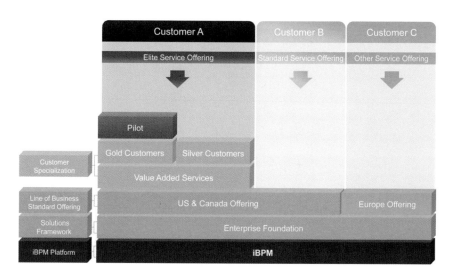

The graphic illustrates the organization of the iBPM assets in reusable layers, each of which contains flows, case types, different types of business rules, decisions, properties, UI, reports, integration, etc. These are the elements that make up executable iBPM solutions. The foundation is the iBPM suite, on top of which you can have multiple layers, reflecting various dimensions that organize the assets. As you move up the layers, you have additional specializations. Layers above reuse (or "inherit" to use a technical, object-oriented term) all of the assets of the layers below. So, typically you start with an enterprise layer that contains the shared assets for the enterprise. You then specialize with additional layers for different lines of business, organizing them through geographical location, type of product, or category of customer. At run-time the underlying iBPM engine will pick the best asset to apply for the given values of the dimensions. This is the essence of iterative excellence, such as applying a discount rule dynamically based on the type of product, customer category, and location.

In other words, the methodology should be corporate asset-building aware. It takes discipline and governance to develop more enterprise-level solutions as opposed to simply building a sliver for a specific problem or objective.

Example: Agile Methodology in Insurance

Vision: An insurance company that insures one million commercial clients and is consistently ranked as a Top 5 carrier by North American property and casualty agents had been focused on expensive business transformation efforts in recent years. The company increased outsourcing and in-sourcing of work to lower cost structures. While these cost savings efforts were successful, they created some unexpected customer service challenges. This new service model created a lot of manual hand-offs, impacted transaction accuracy and elongated customer service cycle time.

Solution: In order to realize its strategic vision, the insurance company focused on a new sprint methodology and used an iterative approach to validate improvement assumptions with business stakeholders before implementation. The company empowered the business to collaborate with their IT counterparts by leveraging iBPM's ability to directly capture business objectives in working application models. This created greater alignment around business challenges and enhanced the company's process redesign improvement opportunities. During this process, the company discovered opportunities to dramatically improve intake across 22 service centers by using intelligent work routing to assign work to the right person and dynamic case management to streamline the policy servicing process.

Results: The insurance company has dramatically reduced service cycle times by deploying a single iBPM solution that provides transparency across channels and manages all customer interactions and history. The company increased first-contact resolution by providing CSRs with guided processes designed to streamline the transaction intake process. iBPM's robust rule capabilities validate transaction information and process work assignments automatically, auto-generates outbound communications to the agent or insured, and points them to a Web page if there is missing information. This enhanced functionality has eliminated costly scanning and indexing costs.

CHAPTER 11

iBPM: The Core of Modern Enterprise Architectures

We discussed a number of architecture concepts in previous chapters. Chapter 5 for instance explained the salient features of SOA and how iBPM is the best way to be successful with SOA initiatives. An enterprise architecture (EA) is the *blueprint* of the enterprise, capturing all the models and their relationships that are needed to associate the strategies and business objectives of the enterprise with operationalized systems and technology infrastructures.

Why do you need an enterprise architecture? The world is changing faster than most enterprises can keep up with. IT projects tend to be late and over budget. IT backlogs are frustrating, both for the business and IT. Sometimes organizations grow with multiple IT units, each with their own applications, infrastructures, and standards. The often chaotic aggregate of legacy applications, systems, and solutions needs robust management, organization, and framework for governance and structure. In most enterprises there is a gap between the business strategy and the underlying technology architectures that need to support the management objectives. There are inconsistencies between business units with little or no sharing of services. Legacy systems and maintenance often sap IT resources, with little budget left to modernize and innovate in order to keep pace with business demands.

Now, more than ever, enterprises need to become more agile to face increasingly demanding customers and constantly changing market conditions. The challenges addressed by enterprise architectures include silos between various functional or business units, regulatory compliance, responding to customer demands, and choreographing with supply chain partners. Enterprise architectures are an attempt to govern the modernization of the enterprise and narrow the gap between management objectives and the underlying operations that are intended to support them. Its goal is to lay a solid foundation for the complexity of the enterprise and aims to handle the requirements for continuous change. Enterprise architectures strive to achieve reuse and sharing of solutions or services across lines of businesses. Through frameworks, methodologies, and end-to-end blueprints for the entire enterprise, EA initiatives attempt to provide transformed and modernized enterprise models. EA initiatives also attempt to provide guidelines and frameworks in order to modernize the enterprise and liberate it from legacy solutions and outdated technologies.

Enterprise Architecture Models

EA initiatives are launched to cope with the complexity of the changes in the business, the dependencies between organizational units, consistency, governance, sharing across business units, and of course the underlying applications and infrastructures that need to support them.

Traditionally there are several categories of models that are captured in enterprise architectures. The four most pervasive ones are:

- Business Architecture: This focuses on the business strategy, the organization of the enterprise, the various services of the business and the core strategic as well as operational processes within the business. The business architecture encompasses the objectives, the business requirements and the business process solutions that are implemented as business applications (typically and increasingly as BPM applications). The business architecture also symbolizes the approaches for innovation and specialization that could easily be achieved by business. Most importantly, the business architecture needs to realize change and agility. Business architectures can involve strategic methodologies and frameworks, such as the balanced scorecard that divides the business vision into four perspectives: customer, financial, internal, and learning perspectives. The business architecture can focus on improving specific measures through leveraging the application, information, and infrastructure architectures. Process excellence and improvement methodologies such as Lean Six Sigma can also be covered by the business architecture.

- **Information Architecture:** The timeliness, analysis, consistency, and overall quality of information manipulated in business processes and application architectures need to be very reliable. Information architectures provide modeling of all entities, their relationships and the comprehensive models of "data" and "information" that are needed to run the enterprise. It includes structured relational database logical and physical models, as well as multi-media document models and repositories. Comprehensive information architectures span data extraction, data transformation, and the governance processes of the enterprise's master data. Information architecture also includes data marts and data warehouses. The data is typically provisioned and aggregated from multiple applications, in schemata that capture dimensions and measures. Data mining and predictive analytics can be used to discover insight from the data.

- **Application Architecture:** In the overall organization of architecture models, application architecture provides the models, the patterns, and the designs of the various software components for business processes. The application architecture blueprints provide all the details of the applications, including how they interact and leverage information models, the interaction and interfaces of applications, and the enterprise application design patterns. Enterprise applications target the support of business objects and run the business. Thus the models also provide the relationships and links to components of the business strategies expressed in business architecture models and complements. In designing applications and their interrelationships, there are a number of design patterns, such as Model, View, and Controller (MVC). As noted, SOA provides another relatively more recent pattern, especially in the context of the service-oriented enterprise that we discussed in Chapter 5.

- **The Infrastructure (Technology) Architecture:** This focuses on the organization of the hardware and core infrastructure software that is required to support the performance, security, and reliability of the enterprise. Typically there will be clusters of servers interconnected over local and wide area networks. Increasingly enterprises are also deploying on the cloud leveraging Infrastructure as a Service (IaaS) to deliver infrastructure resources, such as storage, networking and servers, as a service. Rather than purchasing servers and network equipment, and worrying about data-center space, clients instead buy those resources as fully outsourced services. See Chapter 13 for more information on IaaS.

The point is that all these artifacts are interrelated and modeled, and the focus of the EA initiative is to come up with the miniature model, the blueprint of all these interrelated architecture artifacts. There have been many frameworks and methodologies for enterprise architectures. Some of the more popular ones include the Zachman framework,[33] TOGAF,[34] and the Federal Enterprise Architecture.[35] EA initiatives model the enterprise and attempt to align the IT execution of operations in the enterprise to strategic business goals.

A problem that frequently arises in EA initiatives is that you often get paralysis through analysis—the proliferation of models with many artifacts that cover the entire spectrum of the enterprise. The result is a collection of blueprints and models that take many months to design with no actual execution. It is difficult to achieve alignment to the business strategy when using a pure modeling approach. This is similar to building a miniature model of a house or a building without considering the actual structure/execution and only using the blueprint.

Enterprises and their architectures continue to mature and evolve over time. New paradigms have attempted to capture emerging trends, market realities, and more modern technologies. They have also attempted to move much closer to execution, automation and operationalization vs. pure modeling. There are also cultural changes,

---

[33] Zachman International Enterprise Architecture (2012)."About the Zachman Framework." Accessed in 2012. http://www.zachman.com/about-the-zachman-framework

[34] The Open Group (2011). *TOGAF® Version 9.1*. Zaltbommel, Netherlands: Van Haren Publishing.

[35] United States Congress House of Representatives (2011). *Federal Enterprise Architecture: A Blueprint for Improved Federal IT Investment Management and Cross-agency Collaboration and Information Sharing*. Washington D.C.: BiblioGov.

such as the emergence of social networking that has given tremendous power to the voice of the customer, who needs to be listened and responded to in ever-shorter periods of time. The iBPM philosophy is model-driven development or construction: What you model is what you execute (vs. what you model is what you generate modeling artifacts for.) The iBPM philosophy makes the enterprise agile, unlike traditional EA approaches where the miniature model of the house never gets constructed.

In Chapter 1 we discussed the "B" in iBPM, defined as the business objectives, the business requirements and the business solutions that are implemented as iBPM applications. The "B" also symbolizes the innovations and specializations that could easily be achieved by business. Crucially, the "B" stands for the change and agility achieved through the iBPM suite. These are very similar to the objectives of top-level enterprise architecture.

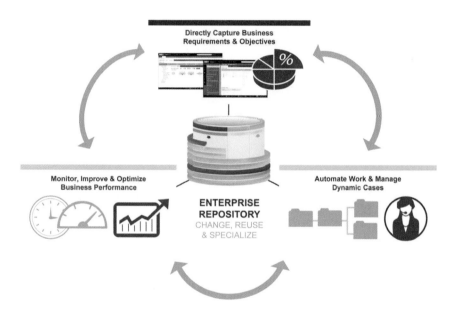

The essential contrast between EA and iBPM is that the latter places emphasis on *dynamic case automation* and *real-time execution* of strategies, rather than spending a lot of time in big-bang projects that design a number of blueprints and miniature models with little or no perceived business value. A better way to characterize iBPM is to think about the actual words "business process *automation*," implying the automation as well as the management of dynamic cases. The iBPM-centric enterprise architecture sticks to our "Think big, but start small" strategy, with emphasis on immediate generation of value. The iBPM architecture focuses on directly capturing the objectives of the business and *executing* these. It also emphasizes the creation of executable models, policies and processes as well as supporting dynamic cases, as discussed in Chapter 9. Finally, the iBPM architecture provides complete visibility into the performance of a certain sector of the business with the ability to drill down, execute and introduce improvements.

Business and IT Gap

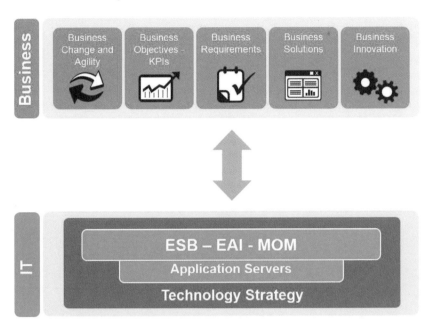

We typically have a gap in many enterprises between the business strategy and the underlying technology strategy or architectures. In addition to the traditional silos between IT and business, organizations face the challenge of change, especially in the current economic climate. Over time, the frequency and magnitude of change increases due to new competition, dissatisfied customers and disruptive technologies. As the rate of change increases, the IT-business gap widens.

Customer and Enterprise Gap

In addition to the vertical gap between business and IT, there is horizontal gap between the voice of the customer and the underlying enterprise with all its solutions, as we discussed in Chapter 6. Social media interactions, exchanges, and feedback need to be an integral part of an umbrella case that involves both internal (to the organization) and external (public social media) sources. When dealing with various channels and customers, enterprises need to remove potential gaps that exist between social networking and inbound front-office customer interactions and the back-office systems that often are required to resolve customer requests, disputes, or feedback. Enterprises are increasingly differentiating themselves through personalized and situational or contextual treatment of customers. This means, for instance customer service interactions will be guided by a comprehensive view of the customer, their individual history with the company, current disposition, how similar customers have been treated, activities that happen within the interaction itself, as well as the feedback gained from social media communications through forums, tweets, and other social media channels. In terms of architecture, there is a gap where the enterprise attempts to respond to the voice of the customer, but ends up diluting the response in siloed, disconnected systems, functional units, lines of businesses, departments, teams and roles.

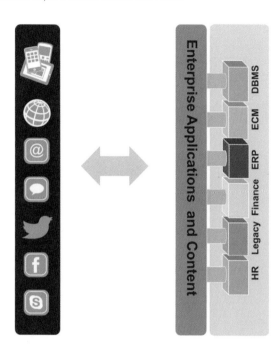

The Modern Business Architecture

The way to resolve and eliminate these gaps is to use an iBPM-focused architecture to bridge the gaps between business objectives and underlying technology architectures. Organizations have high-level objectives and the corresponding specific measurable KPIs to realize those objectives. As illustrated in our discussion of the business-IT and customer-enterprise gaps, many enterprises have lost their leadership (even their existence), as they were too siloed (horizontally and vertically) and late in responding to change.

Enterprises often realize the information that they needed to avoid a crisis or respond to a trend that was available in the data. But the speed of gaining insight from the data and more importantly *operationalizing and acting upon* the insight often lagged considerably.[36] Typically there is too much data stored in different databases and information sources. Big data gathered and aggregated from both enterprise and social media is adding another potential source of opportunities but also challenges. In addition to historic data, enterprises need to monitor and act upon the data generated from the day-to-day operationalized activities of business processes and social media interactions. Through the revamped modern architecture, optimizations need to be performed globally and holistically, strengthening and addressing bottlenecks in the weakest links, while keeping the measurable objectives in control and potentially in real time using iBPM.

In the modern architecture, the underlying technology architecture is important and leveraged extensively by the core iBPM layer. SOA components and capabilities provide the foundational "plumbing" for the business performance and intelligent business process layers of the modern business architecture. Another important trend here is the Infrastructure as a Service (IaaS is discussed in Chapter 13), that provisions the infrastructure on the cloud. Whether on premise or on the cloud, as we saw in Chapter 5, SOA provides the ability to loosely couple applications, trading partners, and organizations and invoke them via service calls. Here again, iBPM is the way to achieve success in service orientation. Therefore, bridging both business-IT and customer-enterprise gaps can be achieved through iBPM, especially with its *dynamic case management* and *analytics* capabilities that treat the customer holistically.

---

iBPM can eliminate the gap from business objectives to execution, as well as the gap from the voice of the customer to the operations in the enterprise. This two-fold (business stakeholder and customer) optimization transforms the way organizations build, deploy, and improve business solutions. Organizations are able to realize the promise of enterprise architecture through the iBPM-enabler engine. Thus KPIs that are obtained from a perspective of the customer as well as finance (as in the balanced scorecard), can be easily connected to process improvement initiatives that are realized through iBPM dynamic case automation projects. iBPM's speed to execution, agility, and adaptability can provide unprecedented advantage in keeping up with a rhythm of change as the objectives of enterprise architecture can be executed and improved continuously.

Example: Financial Institution Reduces Costs +£1Billion

Vision: One of the largest financial institutions in the UK provides general insurance, life insurance, pensions and investment products to over 12 million customers. It is using iBPM as the underpinning for more than 200 projects in the enterprise-wide business transformation program designed to transform its operations and reduce cost by more than £1billion.

Solution: The company launched a major initiative in three phases. The first phase re-engineered processes to reduce touch points, handoffs, chasing, elapsed time, errors and complaints. It introduced a new user interface, the automatic routing of work while increasing multi-skilling and reducing training requirements. iBPM's scalable architecture, combined with a strong governance model, provided the right platform for this project.

Results: The bank reduced more than 700 work types on the legacy solution to 23 core processes, yielding multiple operational benefits. The bank has reduced the number of cases requiring re-indexing by 80%, while the proportion of cases suspended is down by 50%, handoffs have been reduced by 30%, and number of customer touch points reduced by 30%.

 The bank achieved a 10% improvement in productivity in Phase 1. With reusable supporting processes for use with each of the core processes, it expects significant reuse to substantially reduce costs and development time in subsequent project phases. The two subsequent phases will involve interface integration with back-end systems to enable automation and more end-to-end deployment to maximize automation and minimize manual work. The bank expects to achieve a similar 10% productivity improvement in each phase.

CHAPTER 12

iBPM and ECM

This chapter focuses on the relationship between enterprise content management (ECM) and iBPM. ECM is an enterprise software category that manages unstructured content. ECM systems deal with the lifecycle of the documents that can originate from any source or application, such as mobile devices, scanned paper documents, office application documents, e-documents, faxes, e-mails, digital videos, and images.

The scope of document and content management is expansive and strategic as information continues to grow exponentially. In 2012, the total amount of digital information was 2.7 zetabytes, an increase of 48% from the previous year.[37] And how big is a zetabyte? It is 10 to the power 21, compared to a megabyte which is a million bytes—10 to the power 6. A zetabyte is equivalent of a stack of books from Earth to Pluto 20 times over.[38] In other words, very large! In particular, the rate of unstructured content generation—mainly video—is accelerating exponentially, due to social networking, the proliferation of mobile devices, and the advent of cloud computing which we will discuss in Chapter 13. The vast majority of digitized information in the universe is unstructured digital information.

This unstructured content needs to be captured, indexed, managed, organized, accessed (search or navigation), updated (under version control), and leveraged in enterprise business applications and on the Web. ECM also manages the archived versions of documents. That is the crux of enterprise content management. As we shall see in this chapter, iBPM provides the best context and platform for business applications and solutions that involve multiple ECM systems or enterprise content sources. iBPM is the content intelligence and agility layer, both in the creation of content as well as its use and distribution in dynamic case management solutions, as iBPM can leverage, aggregate, and use both structured and unstructured digital information.

Enterprise Content Management Lifecycle

ECM spans the end-to-end lifecycle of documents or unstructured information. The objective is to deliver timely and precise content to decision makers and all categories of workers including transactional, knowledge-assisted workers, and knowledge workers.

---

[37] Wikipedia (2013). "Zettabyte." Last Modified July 29, 2013. http://en.wikipedia.org/wiki/Zettabyte

[38] Evans, Dave (2011). "Ten in Ten: Ten Technology Trends that will Change the World in Ten Years." Paper presented at the Cisco Expo, Kiev, Ukraine, November 1-3, 2011.

Information or "content" can be categorized as *structured* and *unstructured*. Examples of structured information include relational database tables with various columns or fields, such as tables for employees, customers, suppliers, and products. These are managed with Database Management Systems (DBMS), especially relational databases.

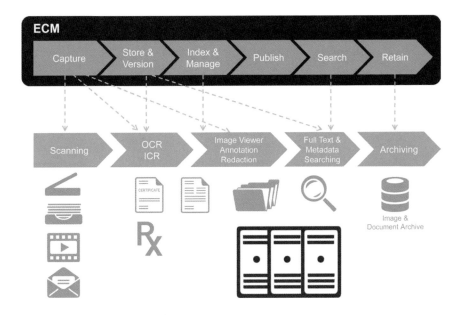

All other types of digital information are examples of unstructured content which constitute more than 85% of an organization's information base. As we have noted, modern-day digital content emanates from a variety of sources, including documents generated by office applications, scanned documents, and a rapidly growing body of multi-media types generated via social networking systems including text, audio, images, and video. ECM spans the lifecycle of all this unstructured digital content, from creating or capturing content and optical character or image recognition to editing, publishing, versioning, indexing, searching and archiving.

ECM and Dynamic Case Management

Unstructured and multi-media documents are essential in many iBPM applications, and especially dynamic case management applications that involve unstructured, collaborative processes. iBPM manages structured, production workflow as well as unstructured and collaborative dynamic cases. The accompanying illustration shows the anatomy of a dynamic case which includes unstructured digital information. This unstructured content can originate from potentially multiple ECM repositories. In fact unstructured content used in the case can be:

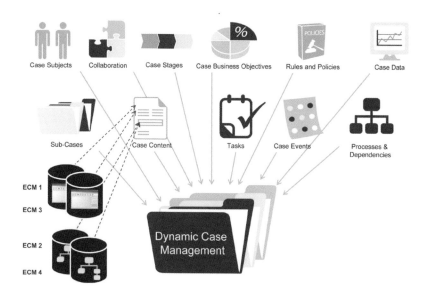

1. Created and managed by the iBPM platform. For instance, an insurance agent can take a picture of an automobile via a mobile phone and that becomes part of the case content, directly attached to and managed by the iBPM case repository.
2. Alternatively, in the context of dynamic case applications, the content can be managed by underlying ECM(s), but accessed seamlessly within the dynamic case. An enterprise typically will have ECMs, with five or more ECM platforms from the same or different vendors not uncommon in large enterprises.

Document Metadata

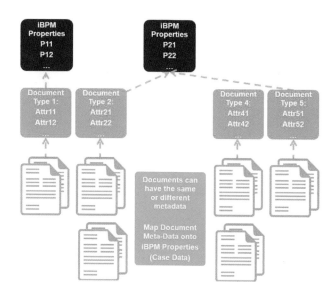

It's important to note that in this second scenario—multiple ECMs—you will have references or document resource links to the documents within the case. While the iBPM manages the processes, the actual documents are stored and managed by the underlying ECM. From an application or resource point of view, this access is transparent: The user searches or navigates to a document and then uses it in the case, without worrying about where it came from or how it is managed.

Multi-media documents have metadata fields or properties. Some of these are built in, such as the author, creation date, date last modified, size and so on. Others could be defined by ECM application developers for specific customer application types. In iBPM applications, there are different types of data. There are built-in attributes that are designed and managed by the iBPM platforms, such as the status assigned to the case of Open, Suspended, or Closed; the creator or originator of the case; the time the case was created; the purpose of the case; and many more. There are also custom fields or properties in the iBPM dynamic case application. For instance, a procurement application will include the originator of the procurement request, the amount, the purpose, as well as the items that need to be procured. In addition to these (potentially structured, complex, or unstructured) fields or properties and documents, the iBPM case can include data from a plethora of sources. Some of these are relational databases (structured) and others are ECM systems (unstructured). Interestingly, almost all iBPM applications involve unstructured data, reflecting the fact that 85% of an enterprise's digitized information is in unstructured format.

iBPM allows data exchange and interoperability with ECMs be seamless, and iBPM properties can be mapped onto the metadata of the documents. For instance, if a document has a customer attribute, say Location, then that field can map automatically to a property of the iBPM dynamic case solution. The value can be used to decide how to route the document in an iBPM decision rule. The documents that become part of the iBPM application's case actually continue to be managed by the underlying ECM while iBPM models and automates the business policies and procedures around the use of these documents.

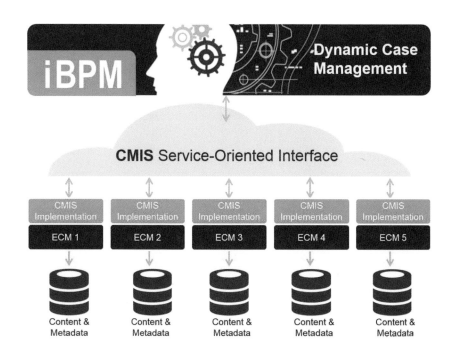

iBPM provides a layer and platform of agility with the ability to aggregate content from multiple ECMs. The Oasis[39] organization has developed a standard application programming interface called Content Management Interoperability Services (CMIS), which is similar to relational database standards such as SQL and standard Java APIs, including JDBC. ECMs use this standard for interoperability, and it is through this standard layer that the iBPM solution can reference one or more ECMs, seamlessly linking to the documents managed by these systems in dynamic cases.

Intelligent BPM for ECM

Documents (including rich media and application documents) are quite common in business process management applications. Here are some examples:

- A loan processing application will include faxes, original signatures, and images of the property as attachments to the form.
- A service processing application will have attachments such as the service agreement, service project sheets, and invoice.
- A compliance application will have the Request for Proposal document, policy documents, and legal attachments.

---

[39] Oasis Content Management Interoperability Services (CMIS) TC (2012). "Oasis Standards." Last Modified June 21, 2012. https://www.oasis-open.org/standards

There is a clear division of roles and functionality between DBMS for structured data, ECM for unstructured data and iBPM for automated cases that create, update, and use both the structured and unstructured data. Knowing the tremendous value that ECM provides to iBPM dynamic case solutions, it is also important to consider the advantages that rules-driven iBPM provides to ECM.

An intelligent iBPM platform allows documents and content managed with ECM tools to be involved in policies as well as practices of the organization to elevate the use and visibility of ECM artifacts. iBPM also allows the content's document and folder metadata to be used in different categories of business rules. Thus decisioning rules, interfacing, and event correlation can be applied to the ECM objects and then used to drive processes with ECM content. For example, in a dispute process, iBPM can be integrated with the ECM system so that the dispute can be resolved, tracked, audited, communicated, and resolved in an expeditious and controlled manner.

In addition to the intelligent business process enablement of ECM, iBPM can be used to manage exceptions, one of the more complex and challenging issues in software engineering. For example, a loan application that is delayed beyond 30 days can launch an exception-handling process that analyzes the loan application phases.

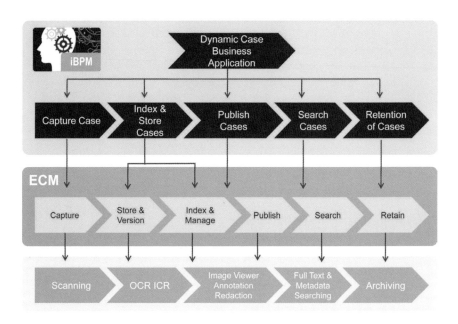

Most large enterprises typically include several federated content repositories. Here the iBPM solution can become the aggregation point for the distributed ECM platform. These repositories can have different levels of support for document retention and streamlining of documents between hierarchical storage module layers. iBPM provides tremendous added value by managing rules pertaining to different repositories through a central, intelligent aggregation point with digitized policies and processes.

We conclude this chapter with four distinct advantages of iBPM for ECM:

- **iBPM Dynamic Case Layer for Document Lifecycles:** As indicated above, content goes through a lifecycle from creation and capture to indexing, storage, and versioning in "published," readily searchable or navigable content repositories. Sometimes the tools and facilities for the enterprise content lifecycle are provided by different vendors, some of which focus on capture, others on storage or content retrieval. Furthermore, an enterprise typically maintains multiple ECMs. Dynamic case management can provide an ideal intelligent, robust, and uniform solution to control the various tasks and phases in document lifecycles as it delivers an agility and modernization layer, while leveraging and integrating with underlying ECM technologies.
- **iBPM Dynamic Cases Integrate Documents from Heterogeneous ECMs:** The workflows in ECM can only process the documents within their own repositories. With dynamic case management, users can create sub-cases that contain documents from different ECM repositories. For instance, a purchasing system for services needs to reference legal documents, license maintenance agreements and support documentation from different systems of record. With iBPM's rich collection of business rule types, you can invoke multiple workflows and use rules-driven integration to drive the invocation as well as the management of work across multiple ECM repositories.
- **iBPM Can Act as the Central Intelligent Aggregation Point for Global Retention Policies:** This means there is a central and separate retention rule set that is managed by iBPM. IT, in collaboration with business stakeholders, can delegate the retention rules to the appropriate owner. More importantly, instead of updating retention policies in different ECM systems or repositories, the iBPM can provide a central governing policy for the entire extended enterprise and enforce regulatory compliance policies. With a common retention policy, there is no need to implement and maintain the retention functionality within multiple ECM products, allowing for flexibility in planning, migrating, or even outsourcing these functions. Policy changes are readily available and can be quickly enforced through periodic updates of the retention parameters for the individual ECM suites.

iBPM Context for Social Networks

iBPM provides the context for social interactions, while at the same time leveraging synchronous and asynchronous social networking capabilities in iBPM solutions. The content management world is changing significantly with the introduction of social interactions and media in the enterprise. Customers and consumers are now accustomed to participating over these social networking channels. Most of what they collaborate, discuss, or exchange ideas about is unstructured, multi-media content, such as videos on YouTube or pictures posted on Facebook. To manage this type of content, modern enterprise software, including iBPM and ECM, are increasingly social-enabled. Even more importantly, within the context of dynamic cases, various types of workers can publish, operate, and interact with public social networks while at the same time leveraging same-time (such as IM, chat, or real-time video) and different-time (such as discussion traces, Facebook, Google+ or Tweets) channels.

Example: Integrating iBPM to Manage Content End-to-End

Vision: A bank sought to drive their "customer first" mission while meeting the ever changing needs of their customers. Several internal studies supported the working theory that loyalty was a key driver of growth. As a result, the bank focused on making it easier for their customer request management process to deliver rapid and predictable responses to clients. Requests arrived through multiple channels (e.g. phone, branch, fax, e-mail) in eight different geographic regions and then went to 14 different service fulfillment groups, each with different systems and processes, and each of the systems had different types of content. This complex web made it challenging to correctly route specific inquiries, set response time expectations and provide updates on existing requests.

Solution: Using iBPM technology, the bank rebuilt an end-to-end resolution process spanning channels and lines of business. With easily navigated screens, coaching tips and step-by-step prompts, the end-to-end resolution process guides users through the complexities of documenting problems. It even immediately resolves cases at the point of service. The process automation capabilities of this new backbone drive higher efficiency rates by automatically retrieving customer data required for resolution, routing cases to the correct support group or individual, and generating supporting forms and correspondence.

Results: The bank's proprietary studies quantified the hard dollar benefit of an improved customer experience. That allowed them to align the project with their "client first" vision instead of just focusing on productivity gains. With enforceable SLAs tuned for each request type, customer segment and fulfillment group, the new end-to-end resolution process presents "high confidence" service commitments. Representatives can now accurately manage expectations and provide expedited service to higher value clients; leading to a better customer experience and a stronger loyalty bond. The automated processes drastically reduced errors and duplicates which allowed the support staff to focus only on the steps that required their skill and judgment. The bank was not only able to decrease the total elapsed resolution time (in some cases down from five days to 30 minutes), but also reduced back-office headcount by 20% in the support organization. When the solution was rolled out to the 30,000+ users, the field adoption rates, with no training for the agents, were greater than 60% for Phase 1. By Phase 2 they had climbed to 80%.

CHAPTER 13

Cloud iBPM

Cloud computing is one of the hottest technology trends of the past decade. Software, platforms, and infrastructures on "the cloud" (which means accessed via the public Internet through a browser or mobile device) are fast becoming the preferred mode of provisioning enterprise software. All of the iBPM capabilities discussed in the previous chapters—both from solution development and execution perspectives—can be on the cloud. iBPM can provide an ideal cloud-based platform to design and build business solutions. For instance, dynamic case management solutions can be built on the cloud, and social collaboration on case design, UI, or business decisioning logic can also be achieved via the cloud. As we shall see in this chapter, there are distinct advantages of cloud computing over traditional on-premise deployments and solutions.

What is Cloud Computing?

Cloud computing is a mechanism that enables users to access various types of services over the Internet (networks, servers, storage, and business applications) conveniently and on demand. There are multiple defining characteristics of cloud computing as follows:

- Deployed Over the Internet/Intranet: This is essential. Cloud computing could as well have been called Internet computing. However, in some (especially large) organizations in the private and public sector, all the advantages of cloud computing are leveraged *within* the firewalls of the enterprise—in other words within the "Intranet"—because of security considerations. This is called *private* cloud in contrast to *public* cloud. Private cloud extends traditional client/server computing (typically with thick-client applications that need to be installed) to mobile app or thin-client, browser-based, provisioning. A large organization can provide all the benefits of on-demand provisioning of solutions within the organization. However, the organization still needs to provide and maintain its own server farms and data centers. So increasingly the term cloud computing is becoming synonymous to *public* cloud computing as opposed to private cloud computing.
- Pay as You Use: Cloud computing is like utilities: You pay for as much as you use. In fact, the analogy extends to the ease of plugging into the fabric of the cloud and then being billed based on the usage of resources. This means the waste that is incurred to purchase and provision on-premise systems or data centers is avoided. Often organizations drink the on-premise software Kool-Aid, only to end up hoarding shelf-ware that does not get used.
- Scalable and Elastic: Cloud computing provides an elastic environment where additional resources can be easily be added as needed for scalability. This is an important advantage of cloud computing because you can easily grow (or shrink) your requirements. It is similar to adding additional phone lines, or increasing your utilities consumption or Internet computing bandwidth—all on demand.
- Multi-Tenancy: Multi-tenancy is often associated with cloud computing. The term comes from apartment rentals. The tenants in an apartment building share many resources, such as security, landscape and parking facilities, to name a few. However, each tenant has his or her own secure and private apartment. Thus resources are shared, without compromising privacy. Multi-tenancy is an architecture where resources, including hardware resources (computing, database, networks) and software resources are shared among multiple customers or tenants. In fact, multi-tenancy is one of the main reasons some large organizations are reluctant to trust the cloud. They are uneasy about the potential security risks when trusting mission-critical data to the cloud. On the other hand, multi-tenancy and shared resources are key reasons that the cloud is relatively inexpensive.
- Business-Friendly Browser and Mobile App Access: Cloud services are accessed over the Internet and increasingly through mobile devices such as tablets and

smartphones. This provides tremendous flexibility in accessing applications and solutions for an increasingly mobile workforce.

- XaaS: There are many categories of services that can be provisioned on the cloud such as Infrastructures as a Service (IaaS), Platform as a Service (PaaS), and Software as a Service (SaaS).

Why Cloud Computing?

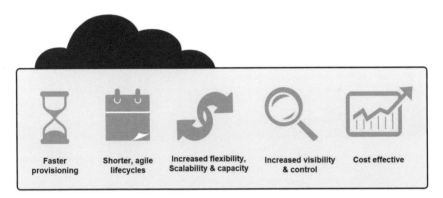

| Faster provisioning | Shorter, agile lifecycles | Increased flexibility, Scalability & capacity | Increased visibility & control | Cost effective |

Cloud computing is becoming extremely popular. By some estimates, the cloud computing market will reach $241 billion by 2020. The cloud software market is growing extremely fast—five times faster than the software market as a whole.[40] There are distinct advantages to cloud computing:

- Provisioning is much faster, whether you are provisioning hardware or business applications.
- The lifecycles of updates or changes to the resources, such as new versions of the software or application, are shorter and more agile.
- Cloud computing enables you to easily scale and add more capacity to handle larger numbers of concurrent users for a business application deployed on the cloud, for example.
- Cloud computing provides increased visibility and control, especially for the business. The business is empowered to select specific business applications and start using them.
- Cloud computing can be much more cost effective since you pay for what you use. The subscription-based, pay-as-you-use model is very attractive to organizations that are struggling financially or at the very least are attempting to control up-front costs of servers, data center rental space, and on-premise software licensing.

---

[40] Robert P. Mahowald and Connor G. Sullivan (2012), "Worldwide SaaS and Cloud Software 2012-2016 Forecast and 2011 Vendor Shares," *International Data Corporation*. http://www.idc.com/getdoc.jsp?containerId=236184

What Type of Service?

As mentioned in our description of cloud computing characteristics, there are many categories of services with IaaS, PaaS and SaaS being the three most common and important.

SaaS

PaaS

IaaS

- **IaaS:** At the bottom you have Infrastructure as a Service which is used to deliver infrastructure resources such as storage, networking and servers as the service. Rather than purchasing servers and network equipment, and worrying about data center space, clients buy these resources as fully outsourced services. There is an important concept that is usually associated with IaaS and that is *virtualization*.[41] The concept of virtualization has been around for a while, used for decades by mainframes to allow multiple operating systems to run on the same hardware server. It also applies to other types of infrastructure resources such storage. Virtualization is used extensively by IaaS providers.
- **PaaS:** Platform as a Service lies between the IaaS and the SaaS types of service. Clients can use a PaaS offering to build complete business applications on the cloud. A PaaS offering can be extensive and include a development environment, testing, deployment, and hosting of the developed application on the cloud. So the entire lifecycle of development is provisioned on the cloud, including collaborative design of processes, business rules, decisioning, reports for activity monitoring, UI, integration, as well as application versioning. The solutions that are tested, designed, and developed on the cloud can target various types of channels, including mobile devices.

---

[41] http://en.wikipedia.org/wiki/Virtualization

- **SaaS:** Software as a Service is perhaps the most popular type of service on the cloud. Here, complete business solutions are accessed on the cloud by clients using Web browsers as well as mobile devices such as tablets or smartphones. The cloud has become a common delivery mechanism for many applications for collaboration, content management, accounting, human resource management and customer relationship management.

iBPM and the Service Models

iBPM can leverage any of these service models to support the development, testing, and deployment of iBPM solutions on the cloud. The two service layers most commonly associated with iBPM are PaaS and SaaS. Here are the options:

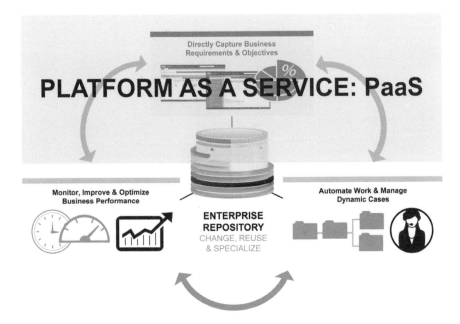

- **iBPM PaaS:** You can provide end-to-end development, testing, as well as deployment of iBPM solutions over the cloud via browsers. iBPM suites are an ideal way to build applications and easily change them on the cloud, making the iBPM platform a PaaS. It is important to note that to make this successful, the unified capabilities of the iBPM suite, including process design, business rules, decisioning, case types, integration, UI development, as well as managing projects and testing, should all be available on the cloud to support a complete business application platform development lifecycle as a service.
- **iBPM SaaS:** Once the application is tested and deployed, it can be accessed as a SaaS on the cloud. This includes the application's dynamic case UI elements, as well as the activity monitoring of the automated cases via browsers and mobile devices. Complete business applications, such as customer service and support,

marketing automation, or claims management can be built as an iBPM solution and deployed on the cloud. Of course, the advantage of building enterprise business solutions with iBPM is the agility—the ability to make changes very quickly—as well as the overall visibility and control of the solution, all of which are augmented by the ease of access enabled by the cloud.

In summary, you can securely build and execute iBPM applications on the cloud. Building the solution and the development lifecycle using an iBPM platform corresponds to PaaS. Once the iBPM solution is built and deployed on the cloud, it becomes a SaaS. Both options can be supported and provisioned on the cloud by iBPM.

When to Use the Cloud: Flexibility through iBPM

When should organizations use cloud computing for their enterprise applications? As mentioned above, cloud computing has a number of distinct advantages, from the speed of provisioning to cost effectiveness.

However, there are reasons for caution. First, cloud computing empowers the business and, as we discussed in Chapter 5, this can lead to "shadow IT" and the presence of solutions within the enterprise that are not formally sanctioned by the enterprise's IT organization and its governance procedures, especially for security. Through cloud computing's flexibility, business can potentially purchase and provision software solutions using their credit cards—bypassing the IT organization altogether.

When it comes to cloud computing, the most serious concern for CIOs is security. Other concerns include availability of the service, performance of solutions deployed on the cloud, and reliability with special concern over losing or corrupting mission-critical data. While all these are legitimate concerns that apply to on-premise solutions, moving applications and mission-critical data to the cloud managed by a third party elevates the enterprise data protection security and reliability risks.

What enterprises need is the flexibility offered through iBPM to overcome these concerns. Both business and IT can achieve their strategic objectives including speed of provisioning, cost reduction, and agility for the business, as well as enforcing security, performance, and reliability policies for IT. iBPM provides the following capabilities for leveraging the cloud in a sensible and secure way:

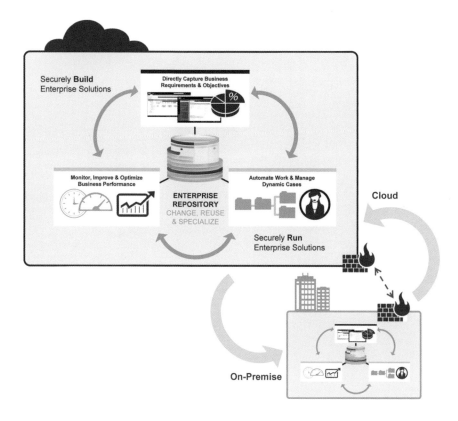

- Development and Testing in iBPM PaaS: You can develop and test on the cloud, and then for security reasons bring the solution on-premise. iBPM platforms allow the integration to be simulated on the cloud, and then the actual plumbing of service or application orchestration can be implemented on-premise. Often cloud solutions need interaction with enterprise applications that are deployed on-premise. In fact, if an application needs constant exchange of data with internal enterprise applications, it might not be a good candidate for production cloud deployment. However, iBPM as a development platform (PaaS) is always a good choice.

- **Deploying on the Cloud: iBPM SaaS:** Increasingly, robust iBPM security solutions on the cloud are supporting industry regulatory standards (such as HIPAA,[42] European Union Data Privacy[43], and others) along with data encryption. Furthermore, service providers are guaranteeing high rates of service availability as well as reliability through mirroring and automatic backup. In other words, as cloud computing matures, increasingly the mission-critical IT governance requirements are addressed, sometimes on par with the standards of on-premise deployments. In addition, it is possible to do secure tunneling and access enterprise applications or data that is deployed on-premise, allowing iBPM applications to be cloud-based. This flexibility of moving between on-premise and cloud is an essential value of cloud-enabled iBPM.
- **Move to the Cloud:** The flexibility for capturing the iBPM solution assets and their portability means you can also take an iBPM solution currently deployed on-premise and move it to the cloud. This option can be especially attractive in freeing the enterprise from the maintenance of data centers as it enables the infrastructure to be outsourced to the cloud service provider.

Hybrid solutions and options for different categories of iBPM solutions are also possible. Furthermore, mature mission-critical iBPM cloud solutions support private cloud options with the enterprise having their own secure operating system, database, web servers, and so forth. In other words, advanced and mature cloud iBPM solutions are allowing enterprises to address the agility requirements of the business and yet still comply with the stringent security and reliability governance policies of IT.

Example: Fast, High-Volume Entertainment Delivery through the Cloud

Vision: In the supply chain world, time is money. Controlling the most market share, this large entertainment company faced the challenge of addressing the growing complexities of its global supply chain in very little time. Its supply chain spans across multiple geographies and languages, and across a mounting array of new channels and media formats. Anything that helps the business shorten lead times and reduce the effort and costs of getting products to market is a huge advantage, given that each title may have tens if not hundreds of product variables. The solution had to be available on demand in a cloud-based deployment that would allow the company to get to market quickly and scale the solution over time.

Solution: The entertainment company deployed a cloud-based iBPM case management solution that is tightly integrated with their previously existing supply chain solution. Via the cloud, the company easily and quickly receives data from suppliers while maintaining robust data security, enabling low up-front costs and low risk for management. Dynamic case management empowers business users and allows them to maintain tighter control of all processes as users can see the entire international supply chain and have the flexibility to specialize the delivery process. Developing and deploying on the cloud enabled the delivery team to bring the solution live in just nine weeks, just in time to meet a holiday deadline and provide delivery partners with an easy, secure integration.

Results: The entertainment company anticipates it will save £5 million per year from efficient operations (lower freight costs, transportation expenditures, and improved restock calculations) and superior time management. The company can now make blockbuster releases available to its largest distributors in advance, expanding the profitability of each release. It has met aggressive sales targets for high volumes of product. For example, it recently shipped over six million copies of a video game in just two months, with the titles landing in stores on the same day, worldwide.

CHAPTER 14

iBPM-Enabled CRM for Customer Centricity

iBPM is for customer centricity. What exactly does that mean? It means the needs, expectations, and overall experience of the customer drive the processes and policies of the organization. Very few companies are really customer centric, which is not surprising given most commercial organizations are driven by profit. However, there is a direct link between commercial success and customer centricity. In a very real sense, this chapter is the culmination of the previous chapters when it comes to the value proposition of iBPM. As we shall see, iBPM-enabled customer relationship management (CRM) provides tremendous opportunity to operationalize and optimize the customer experience in order to increase profitability.

Measuring the Customer Experience

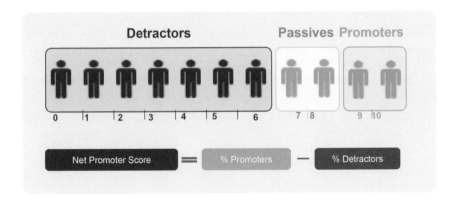

How does a company know it is providing an excellent customer experience? Of course, the actual financial success of the commercial enterprise is one obvious measure. While revenue will eventually make or break a company, there are other measures that are much better predictors of the organization's customer centricity and overall success (or failure). One of the most robust measures for assessing the experience of the customer has been the Net Promoter Score (NPS).[44] Introduced by Fred Reichheld in 2003, it is fundamentally a single-question assessment or survey about a customer's willingness to recommend a

---

[44] Net Promoter Score, Net Promoter and NPS are registered trademarks of Bain & Company, Satmetrix Systems, and Fred Reichheld.

product or company to his or her network of friends and acquaintances. The score is on a scale 0-10. Promoters are those who scale 9-10.

With iBPM-enabled CRM, especially customer service and support, organizations can keep their NPS (or other) measures critical to the customer experience in control *in real time*. This is very much a Lean Six Sigma optimization challenge and, as we discussed in Chapter 9, iBPM is an ideal platform to monitor and control all process and performance measures as well as proactively handle potential challenges also in real time.

What is CRM?

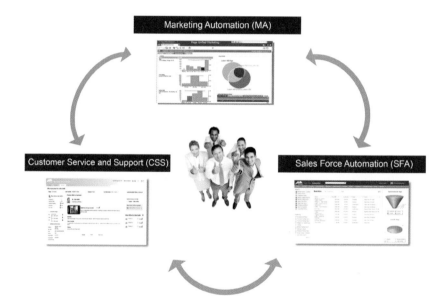

CRM is about managing the relationship between a company that is offering products or services and their customers. CRM involves marketing the company's offerings, selling them, providing customer service and technical support, and up-selling and cross-selling further products or services to existing customers. CRM is automated and operationalized through three essential components:

- **Marketing Automation** provides solutions for marketing lifecycles—from planning marketing programs, to the design and execution of inbound and outbound marketing campaigns—via multiple channels.
- **Sales Force Automation** solutions manage the stages in a sales process including following up on leads generated by the marketing campaigns,

building the relationship with the customer, assigning accounts, and eventually closing the sale.

- **Customer Service and Support** solutions assist customers, through processing their claims, solving problems, answering questions, and responding to their requests. Service and support is provided through multi-channel contact centers and self-service websites or mobile apps. Service and support solutions can also cross-sell and up-sell to existing customers. This is important, as it is well known that it costs a company about six times more to sell a product to a new customer than to an existing customer.

Evolution of CRM

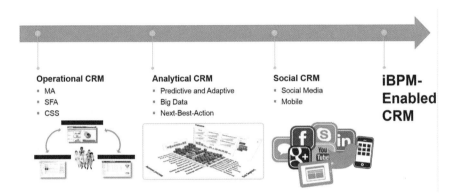

Operational CRM
- MA
- SFA
- CSS

Analytical CRM
- Predictive and Adaptive
- Big Data
- Next-Best-Action

Social CRM
- Social Media
- Mobile

iBPM-Enabled CRM

There have been a number of significant trends and milestones in the evolution of CRM. One of them is analytics, especially predictive and adaptive models leveraged in marketing and sales, as well as in service and support. As we discussed in Chapter 4, predictive techniques can be used to gain insight from market trends and customer behavior, and these discovered models can be operationalized and automated in iBPM solutions. With the ability to learn from the market and customer behavior during a specific customer interaction, analytics is a useful tool to strategize the Next-Best-Action[45] for a specific customer, taking into consideration the individual's background as well as transaction and/or interaction history.

Social networking has also had a profound effect on CRM, as it has given customers a powerful voice, allowing them to instantly provide feedback (good and bad) and share ideas about products, services, and companies. As we discussed in Chapter 6, listening to and communicating with customers via social channels is now critical for success.

With iBPM-enabled CRM, companies can leverage both the analytics and social networking that have profoundly affected managing the customer relationship,

---

[45] http://en.wikipedia.org/wiki/Next-best-action_marketing

enabling organizations to deliver targeted marketing promotions, optimized and automated sales processes, and guided service interactions. Predictive and adaptive analytics in iBPM let organizations learn, discover, and then operationalize predictive models in marketing, sales, and customer service. With adaptive analytics, the decision strategy for the customer continuously learns and adapts to changes in customer behavior or market dynamics. iBPM also enables organizations to dynamically analyze and respond with the right action for each customer. Customers can be heard and responded to through holistic and dynamic cases involving all participants who are needed to resolve the case.

When CRM components and capabilities are built on top of an iBPM platform, they inherit all the advantages of iBPM—process centricity, visibility, control, and transparency into the CRM policies and procedures, as well as the key capability to easily adapt, introduce change, and be agile.

iBPM-Enabled CRM for Customer-Centric Transformation

There is important technology as well as cultural trends that are influencing the transition from traditional CRM to iBPM-enabled CRM. The new generation of customers are quite tech savvy as they leverage social media extensively and expect instant change. They also want to be treated differently, based on their history, background, or situation. iBPM-enabled CRM supports each of these customer trends as it enables organizations to go from:

Traditional Approach	Paradigm Shift	iBPM-Enabled CRM
Data Forms Driven	Intuitive	Process and Intent Driven
Commodity Services	Differentiated	High Value, Situation Specific
Manual Processes & Hand-offs	Work Automation	Dynamic Case Management
Ossified and Hidden Policies and Procedures	Transparency, Visibility, And Customization	Agile, Build for Change
Front – Back Office Silos Customer Enterprise Silos Channel Silos	Customer Centric	Integrated, Unified, and Adaptive
Inside Out and Product Focused Voice of the Enterprise	Social Networking	Voice of the Network
Historic Data Reports	Insightful: Analyze, Learn and Apply	Predictive and Adaptive Decisioning – Next-Best-Action

- Confusing data-driven forms to intuitive processes, decisions and guided interactions.

- Commodity services to delivering tailored, personalized treatments using situational execution to take into consideration such factors as the customer, service, product, reason for the interaction, and geographical location in order to execute the business logic.
- Manual work with manual handling of exceptions to holistic, end-to-end automation through dynamic case management. Dynamic case management also connects the front and back office to deliver a consistent customer experience across multiple channels. Sub-cases handled by different teams or organizations are all aggregated through the holistic case to meet a specific customer objective.
- The "black box" of traditional CRM packages that hides the business logic and is very difficult to change, extend, or customize to complete transparency and visibility of all the procedures, policies, and decisions within the CRM solution that simplify change, maintenance, and customization.
- Product and enterprise focus to customer-centric recommendations based on customer needs and the lifetime value of the customer.

Optimizing the Customer Experience

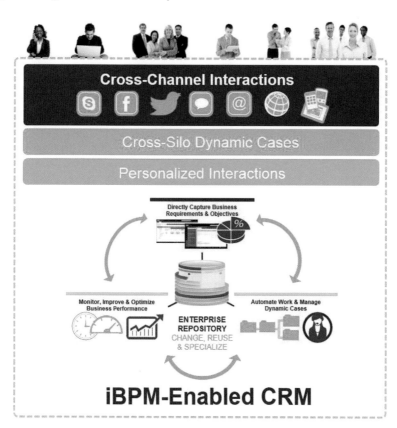

iBPM and its ability to engage in continuous improvement provides distinct and important advantages to optimize the customer experience. With the various operationalized CRM components driven by iBPM, organizations can:

- **Seamlessly Manage the Multi-Channel Experience:** The customer can start an interaction in one channel, such as a mobile device, and continue without interruption in another channel, say the Web or on the phone with a customer service representative. The entire context and the end-to-end case of the customer interaction are maintained across the channels.
- **Act as One Company to the Customer:** Because case management can include multiple sub-cases involving different teams, departments, or units within the enterprise, dynamic case management allows the coordination and collaboration of multiple participants—all working together to meet the customer objective. This holistic aggregation is essential for transforming the customer experience.
- **Personalize Interactions:** iBPM allows different customers to be treated differently. For example, depending on the value of the customer, product, location or service, the most appropriate discount can be offered. Analytics is leveraged for the Next-Best-Action for the customer. In addition, with iBPM, the business has complete visibility to make changes to policies or procedures that affect customer treatments across the customer lifecycle.

iBPM Analytics and Next-Best-Action for CRM

It's worth spending a few minutes looking at how to use iBPM analytics and Next-Best-Action to optimize customer experiences in a little more detail. As we defined earlier, Next-Best-Action leverages real-time decisioning using predictive models, adaptive models and business rules to identify optimal ("best") actions in iBPM solutions.

One of the best ways to optimize the customer experience is to leverage the analytical insight that can be mined from data to support decisioning for the customer. This applies to marketing, sales automation, and perhaps most importantly, customer service. The sources of the decisioning strategy emanate from:

- Business rules that are authored by experts or knowledge workers
- Demographic, census, or other externally sourced data
- Transactional data from the enterprise information systems within the organization
- Data warehouses and data marts that aggregate data from many sources

Business rules are authored as explicit, discrete, and static knowledge provided by experts. Often these are captured in rule books or various policy and procedure manuals. Any of the iBPM rule types, such as decision trees, decision tables, constraints, and expressions, can be used to optimize the experience by driving the processes and dynamic cases to resolution.

Businesses have many hidden treasures in their systems, such as data held in operational databases, data warehouses and even census or publicly available data. There is value in the individual data sources, but even more so in the combination of them. Customer purchase patterns, satisfaction drivers, and future behavior can be uncovered in this data and used to tailor the customer experience.

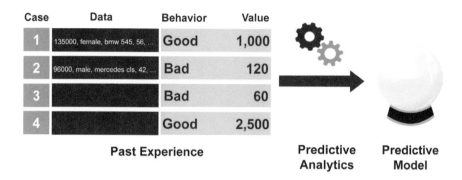

Case	Data	Behavior	Value
1	135000, female, bmw 545, 56, ...	Good	1,000
2	96000, male, mercedes cls, 42, ...	Bad	120
3		Bad	60
4		Good	2,500

Past Experience   Predictive Analytics   Predictive Model

The whole purpose of and motivation for predictive analytics is to discover these patterns, use them to predict future behavior, and then act on the insight. As we have discussed in Chapter 4, predictive analytics is the science behind mining data for repeatable patterns that are reliable enough to serve as a basis for predicting the future. Such a reliable, repeatable pattern, when found, can power a crystal ball that will improve many business decisions, and embedding models in customer processes offers a particular fertile area. For example, you can use predictive models to reach out, proactively, to customers who are likely to churn, buy, or default.

Adaptive analytics, which looks at a moving window of data as it enters the system, offers further opportunity to increase the personalization, relevance, and value of the interaction to the customer. Analytics should result in models that can be enacted and deployed, especially in iBPM solutions. Therefore, the power of predictive and adaptive (or rather *static* predictive and *adaptive* predictive models, as both categories predict future behavior), is realized in iBPM solutions that leverage the discovered predictive models, augmented by business rules and the context of the process. This enables human participants, such as customer service representatives, to make better decisions to cross-sell, up-sell, retain, collect, or service through prioritized Next-Best-Action recommendations.

With iBPM-enabled CRM, the complete spectrum of decisioning is supported—predetermined from the minds of knowledge workers and experts; predictive models discovered from historic data; and decision strategies that learn and adapt to changes in customer behavior or market dynamics. Customer behavior can change because of demographic trends, legislation, interest rates, or a myriad of other factors. Similarly, competitive offers or pricing can stir things up and impact how customers behave. Rather than trying to re-calibrate predictive models manually—forever testing and re-developing updated versions when a model becomes less accurate—adaptive systems update automatically without human intervention.

Customer-Centric Enterprise Architecture

Chapter 11 explained why the best way to achieve and realize the objectives of the business strategy is to make iBPM the core of the overall enterprise architecture. With CRM, the objective is to become customer centric and address specific performance indicators pertaining to customers, such as Net Promoter Scores. iBPM bridges the gap between CRM performance measures and underlying implementations across marketing, sales, and service.

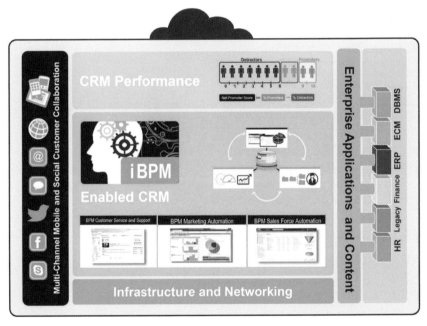

In addition, as we have discussed, iBPM is optimal to address the gap between the voice of the customer, heard through either social networks or inbound communications, and the underlying enterprise with all its solutions. Recall in Chapter 6 where we discussed the relationship between iBPM and social networking. Again, the point is that we have a gap where the enterprise attempts to respond to the customer's voice, but often the response needs dynamic case management to aggregate or provide an umbrella where various lines of business, departments, teams, and roles can respond to the customer's issue. The gap will only close if dynamic case management is employed, enabling the organization to align itself with the voice of the customer and eliminate all the internal enterprise silos using iBPM.

Finally, as we pointed out in Chapter 13, the flexibility of moving between on-premise and cloud deployments is an essential requirement for many enterprises leveraging iBPM for their CRM solutions. Thus, any of the three components of CRM can be developed and deployed on the cloud or on-premise, and the organization can easily move between these two deployment options, or design and develop in one, such as the cloud and move the solution into the other, such as on-premise.

Example: iBPM-Enabled CRM for Warranty Management

Vision: A leading warranty provider had a number of business challenges in its warranty management processes. It wanted to increase sales, lower the cost of services, and improve overall operational efficiencies. The company had just 90 days to implement a new, flexible contact center solution to support the contract. The solution and migration had to be seamless, with zero impact on the customer service representatives' (CSR) ability to service existing contracts. The company needed to integrate the CSR desktop with existing customer and contract data sources, as well as the retailer's systems for original purchase

details and replacement product fulfillment. This process had to be easy to repeat for all new clients, and support unique processing requirements and branding each time. The solution had to provide a seamless, branded experience for the end customer, but ensure CSRs had a consistent and familiar user interface in order to maximize efficiency.

Solution: The company implemented an iBPM-enabled CRM solution and achieved all of their business objectives in just 70 days. The project required just four members of the IT team to complete. A company executive indicated that building the same capability with traditional approaches would have taken at least two or three times as long with three times the resources.

Results: While a large new client was the impetus for the iBPM-enabled CRM solution, it has now been rolled out to all of the company's retail clients, across its seven national contact centers. The company is well positioned for future growth, and their ability to bring new clients on board in less than three months is a key differentiator in winning contracts with major international retailers. The enhanced case management, process automation, and integration with retailers' systems have significantly decreased time to resolve customer inquiries and improved customer service levels. The company reports high levels of satisfaction across all clients.

CHAPTER 15

Pega iBPM—The Next Wave for Customer-Centric Business Applications

This book has shown how intelligent iBPM has matured and evolved to become a viable platform for business applications. iBPM is often touted as a management discipline for improving processes and as a technology that supports agility and change through automation. It is, of course, both. However, the most important value proposition of iBPM is *intelligent automation*. With intelligent capabilities in a unified platform, iBPM becomes the core of the modern business architecture.

Pegasystems has developed Pega iBPM as the next-generation platform to *Build for Change®* agile solutions involving the collaboration of business, operations, and IT. With the Pega iBPM platform, you can easily build and adapt customer-centric solutions that involve automated processes, decisions, interfaces, and end-to-end enterprise integration with zero code! The innovative and transformative capabilities of Pega iBPM have led analysts to recognize Pegasystems as the world's leader in intelligent Business Process Management.

Best of Build and Buy for Transformational, Innovative, and Adaptive Applications

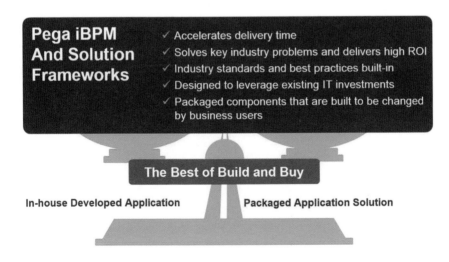

How do organizations deploy applications to keep up with the increasing demands of business stakeholders and continuous change? How can they become agile *and* innovative? Perhaps most importantly, how can they achieve pragmatic business transformation?

Traditionally, there have been two approaches. One is to build the application in-house, using a technology stack with custom coding done by the IT organization, off-shoring, or a combination of both. The problem with this approach is that it is costly, difficult to maintain, and solidifies siloed roles of business stakeholders and IT. Another problem is that industry best practices are not leveraged, and all requirements need to be custom built, in-house. Coding and technology stack development tools do not lend themselves to agility, visibility by the business, or business control.

The other end of the spectrum is to deploy a point or packaged solution. While it is true that packaged solutions do have industry best practices and can typically address stakeholder needs up front, they provide little to no visibility into the internal "black box" policies or procedures that are ossified in the solution. Sometimes, organizations start with a packaged solution and then end up spending considerable resources to customize and change it to their needs through custom code. Thus, organizations attempt to satisfy conflicting objectives—the need to start quickly with industry best practices out-of-the-box, while also needing transparency, visibility, and agility in a consistent platform that is palatable to both business and IT.

This chapter explains how Pega iBPM solves this dilemma. All the characteristics and capabilities of iBPM described in the previous chapters are realized through Pega's new way of building business applications that eliminates the problems of packaged solutions or custom coding. The compelling need to have an agile business platform that leverages industry best practices, satisfies business objectives, and provides visibility and control is exactly the realm of Pega iBPM, which provides the next wave for building business applications.

Pega iBPM for Customer Centricity

Businesses are driven to innovate by rapidly introducing new products, opening new markets, quickly adapting to customer demands, overcoming competition, and complying with new regulations. The need to change emanates from the need to improve process efficiency, eliminate waste, increase the percentage of value work, and keep processes under control in order to optimize customer experiences. For customer-centric organizations, the business objectives are aligned with customer experience optimization. However, operationalizing customer centricity has been a challenge for most organizations, largely because the traditional software lifecycle is a heavy development process with long and complex requirements for deployment. Furthermore, in conventional software development, making changes is arduous and error-prone. At the same time, market pressures, regulatory agencies, global competition, and internal communication challenges drive management to constantly evolve the rules of the business. As time goes on, these evolutionary changes migrate further from the original intent of policies and practices, creating greater impact and increased frequency of change.

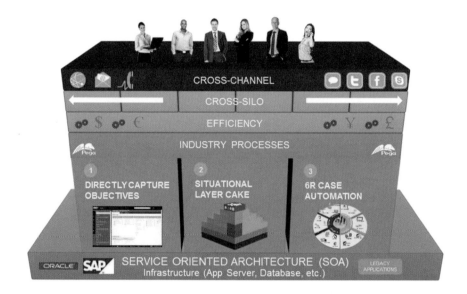

Pega is the world's leading iBPM solution for customer-centric business applications. Pega has achieved this level of prominence by providing comprehensive decision management capabilities in one cohesive platform, including a rich collection of rule types as well as predictive, real-time decisioning for Next-Best-Action marketing, sales automation and customer service and support. Pega easily supports complex customer strategies that can involve scorecards, decision rules, and powerful predictive and adaptive models.

In a world where managing change is now mission critical, Pega iBPM, enables stakeholders to keep up with and control change, especially for KPIs that focus on customer value. Pega iBPM's modern *Build for Change*® platform provides *all* of the capabilities that we have discussed in this book including:

- Business Rules and Decisioning (Chapter 4)
- SOA and Modernization with iBPM (Chapter 5 and 7)
- Social iBPM (Chapter 6)
- Mobile iBPM (Chapter 6)
- Process Excellence and Improvement iBPM (Chapter 8)
- Dynamic Case Management (Chapter 9)

- Transformational iBPM (Chapter 10 and 11)
- Enterprise Content Modernization with iBPM (Chapter 12)
- Cloud iBPM (Chapter 13)
- iBPM-enabled CRM (Chapter 14)

Pega iBPM delivers four essential capabilities that allow organization to rapidly create comprehensive, end-to-end, customer-centric solutions:

- Business Profiler
- Directly Capture Objectives
- Situational Layer Cake
- 6R Case Automation with Dynamic Case Management

Business Profiler: From Business Objectives to Execution

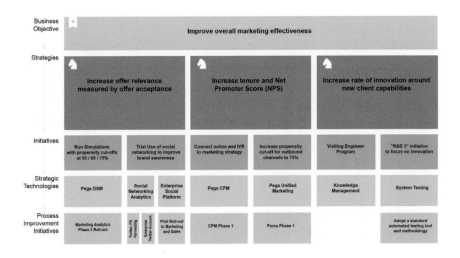

Pega's *Business Profiler*™ allows business stakeholders to align high-level, measurable strategies to process improvement initiatives realized though Pega iBPM. The Business Profiler engages the business and empowers them to capture their business objectives and measurable KPIs in Pega applications. It provides an intuitive organization of the business. Through the Business Profiler, stakeholders can organize and map the strategies in layered, top-down hierarchies from business objectives all the way to Pega iBPM solutions with detailed metrics, checklists, and timelines. The contextual collaboration Pega tool, PegaPulse, aids this process, as it can be used to conduct discussions and feedback conversations around the strategies, goals, and objectives.

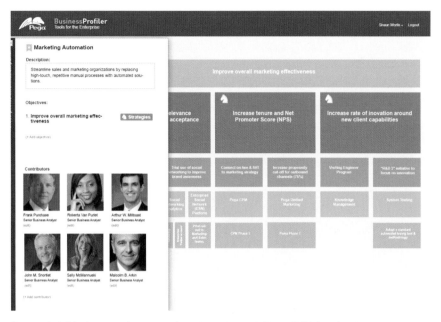

Strategic initiatives can be operationalized through Pega iBPM technologies and solutions. Strategies—the layer below the overall business objective—involve metrics and measurements that are kept up to date in real time. These KPIs can be sourced either from Pega iBPM solutions or external systems. The metrics are real-time

measures that are obtained through standard interfaces (REST). This allows the business stakeholder to always have up-to-date, real-time data on the performance of their strategic initiatives. The KPIs can also be organized in various perspectives (customer, financial, internal, and innovation/growth, as in the balanced scorecard.)[46] The complete visibility into the performance of strategic KPIs, combined with the ability to drill down from KPIs to automated and operationalized Pega iBPM solutions and effect changes for improvement is transformational.

Directly Capturing Business Objectives

The strategies and the corresponding business solutions supporting business strategies, which are identified using the Business Profiler, are operationalized through Pega's *Directly Capturing Objectives* (DCO) constructs. DCO essentially realizes the promise of model-driven development in which working application models are created directly from business mandates. DCO enables far more efficient development of solutions that directly reflect the organization's goals for customer centricity.

If business people are to "own the change," they must be able to close the gap between business objectives and operations. This requires sharing ideas with operations and IT at all stages of an iBPM project to ensure that the solution meets business needs. DCO is the set of capabilities in Pega iBPM that lets business users capture, organize, and manage information directly in the system instead of using disconnected documents or artifacts that are out-of-date or obsolete before the solution is even delivered.

---

[46] See for example: https://www.balancedscorecard.org/

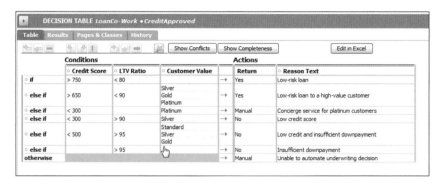

DECISION TABLE	LoanCo-Work	• CreditApproved			

Table | Results | Pages & Classes | History

Show Conflicts | Show Completeness | Edit in Excel

	Conditions			Actions	
	○ Credit Score	○ LTV Ratio	○ Customer Value	Return	○ Reason Text
○ **if**	> 750	< 80		→ Yes	Low-risk loan
○ **else if**	> 650	< 90	Silver Gold Platinum	→ Yes	Low-risk loan to a high-value customer
○ **else if**	< 300		Platinum	→ Manual	Concierge service for platinum customers
○ **else if**	< 300	> 90	Silver	→ No	Low credit score
○ **else if**	< 500	> 95	Standard Silver Gold	→ No	Low credit and insufficient downpayment
○ **else if**		> 95		→ No	Insufficient downpayment
otherwise				→ Manual	Unable to automate underwriting decision

Pre-built case types, forms, and models for process and business-rule logic make it easy for business users to define processes, rules interfaces, new case types and the other essential elements of a solution. This business-focused approach solves the problems of traditional development methods as Pega iBPM enables seamless integration of business objectives in new and evolving solutions; provides business, IT, and operations with full transparency and visibility into all the elements of a business solution; and delivers a thin-client (browser-based) platform as the common language. The unified environment automatically generates the solution from requirements without cumbersome hand-offs, imports and exports between tools, conversion to execution environments, or rebuilding details in multiple environments. Change is fast, but controlled; continuous, but orchestrated.

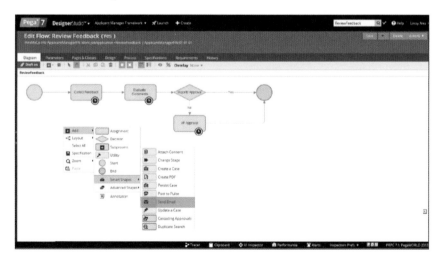

As a result, DCO helps avoid requirements gaps introduced in custom software projects, where business intent is often misunderstood, technical changes obsolete requirements, business needs change during long delivery times, and the business does not have any opportunity to see or provide feedback on the application until it is too late. All these challenges are avoided with DCO, which is accessible to business owners, analysts, designers, and developers. Process maps are easily designed with the Web-based process modeling tool; changes are reflected consistently; and there is never the need for translation, to make a change. Changes and prior versions are automatically tracked, and accesses, as well as change permissions, are controlled for complete application governance.

There are several constructs in Pega iBPM that allows organizations—both the business and IT—to capture their objectives. These include stage-based case design (discussed below), high-level process diagrams, easy-to-use forms for business rules, and of course, more detailed process flow diagrams with built-in, extensible shapes. Pega is 100% model driven—what you model is what you execute and automate. Because Pega iBPM provides accelerators, wizards and visual forms to define application assets in business terms, all aspects of business requirements are modeled and executed directly in the shared environment. Pega solutions can be created and changed using any agile or iterative methodology the enterprise may have adopted.

In addition, business stakeholders can generate documentation as needed during the life of a Pega iBPM solution. Through Pega's innovative "continuous documentation" feature, the requirements document of the solution can be automatically generated from the directly captured models for processes, case types, business rules, UI, and so forth at any time in the process, showing all aspects of the application from requirements and policies and procedures to user interfaces, case models, and integration. Because this documentation is generated directly from the rules on demand, it is always up-to-date and in sync with the actual implementation.

Specialize at Run-Time: Situational Execution

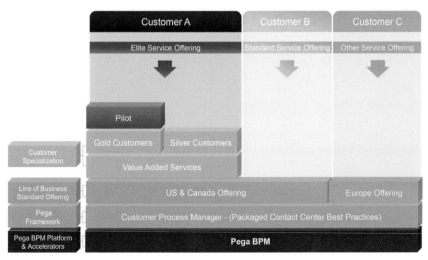

Organizations can respond rapidly to marketing pressures using Pega's unique and patented situational layer cake (SLC), which allows businesses to easily introduce change and specialize for particular situations. Through SLC's run-time specialization, organizations can execute policies and procedures contextually to individualize the treatment for each customer. Pega maintains all the SLC assets developed for enterprise applications (process flows, business rules, decisions, UI, integration, etc.) in its robust and dynamic multi-dimensional repository.

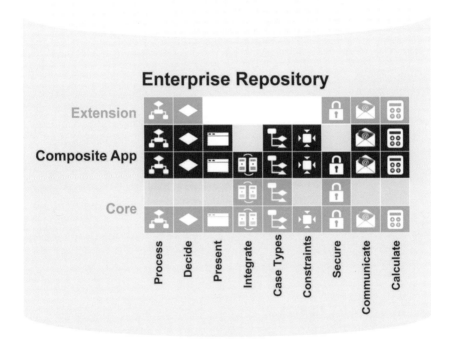

Why SLC? Business applications execute within a context or business intent, such as the type of customer, location, or specific product. There is always a context, and leveraging this context enhances the quality and efficiency of the interaction. With context, the best policy, offer, user interaction, or information source for a given situation can be identified and executed.

The Pega iBPM platform reflects the way people manage situations in business, using the context and business intent to drive the process. The core of Pega iBPM is the enterprise repository of the assets for the business application, such as processes, decision rules, constraints, expressions, user interactions, and integration. Pega iBPM supports:

- Optimized reuse of assets so that certain policies and procedures can be shared across lines of businesses or within the enterprise;
- Specialization of assets for specific types of customers, geographical locations, or products and services; and then
- Automatic situational execution of the most appropriate specialized asset (policy or procedure) for a given situation.

Out-of-the-box, the repository supports versioning, auditing, access control, testing, search, navigation, and processes for managing change. Using this repository, an organization can create common policies and procedures, and then add specialization layers for specific situations that allow it to treat different customers differently. Pega iBPM makes it easy to reuse, specialize, and then situationally execute for a given business scenario or interaction.

For example, when a customer service organization needs to add variation to accommodate a new product group, line of business, or channel, it only needs to build the deltas on top of the Pega iBPM foundational policy and procedure layers, which are already defined. There will be standard discount policies that are the default across all products, jurisdictions, or customers. Then, there will be specializations of the discount policy. For instance, a different discount calculation could be expressed as a specialization to reflect a certain type of the customer or state regulation, enabling change to be easily managed.

Pega calls this *run-time specialization* and it achieves contextual execution through Pega's situational layer cake where sets of policies and procedures are built as layers on top of one another. Each layer inherits business logic from the lower layers. Pega iBPM dynamically selects and executes the most specialized policies and procedures from the layer cake based on the situation.

This unique layering capability is at the core of the Pega iBPM architecture, and run-time specialization is a revolutionary approach that eliminates the need for extensive coding or manual human intervention to handle the exceptions that are so often the rule. Instead, a simple specialized layer captures the rules for each particular situation and automatically executes them with the situation is right.

6R Case Automation with Dynamic Case Management

At the very core of Pega iBPM is automation of the work to handle cases from end-to-end. Pega iBPM achieves this through **receiving** work from multiple channels, **routing** it to the most qualified resources, and **reporting** on it through monitoring actionable reports. Via its intelligent and unified business rules and decisioning capabilities, Pega solutions support **researching** for just-in-time information, **responding**, and **resolving** the dynamic cases. Pega calls this *6R case automation*.

| Processes & Dependencies | Case Type | Business Objectives | Stages | Rules & Policies |
| Case Data | Case Subjects | Content | Sub-Cases | Case Events | Tasks |

Recognized by analysts as the leading *dynamic case management* platform, Pega iBPM supports dynamic work automation in business applications from end-to-end through its 6R work automation capabilities. Pega iBPM also supports all types of workers including clerical workers, knowledge-assisted workers, and knowledge workers. More importantly, Pega's dynamic case management adapts to the way the business defines and monitors its milestones and progress. Leveraging the situational layer cake, it dynamically tailors each task or interaction of the case, and supports dynamic case content, as discussed in Chapter 9. The case work gets resolved by automating wherever possible and guiding users when human involvement is needed. For example, a Pega solution can automate correspondence generation to minimize effort and ensure consistency. It can support the definition, subscription, and robust handling of business events. A Pega iBPM application can also keep track of all the business activities and allow business users to drill down to control the performance of the solution.

Of key importance is Pega's ability to automate structured and predetermined processes, as well as ad-hoc tasks, executed in the context of dynamic cases. The events, responses, and resolution of the case are all automated through the Pega iBPM solution.

Pega dynamic case management supports:

- **Case Lifecycle Management for Business Stakeholders:** Case Lifecycle Management mirrors the way business people think, defining work in terms of milestones towards a strategic objective. Pega calls these *stages* and allows the business to directly define the stages, as well as all the processes that need to be executed for the stage. This unique and innovative design allows business stakeholders to organize their cases into distinct milestones.

  Consider the stages required when onboarding a new employee. For each stage, there are sub-cases or processes and corresponding tasks that need to be executed and completed. The transition from one stage to the next can be done automatically or manually by the case manager or worker. These are clearly depicted in the stage design. For example, when a chevron arrow icon is used to represent moving to another stage, it means the system will automatically transition the case from this stage to the next one once all of the first stage's processes and tasks are completed. If there is a straight line between two stages, it means the transition is done manually by the case worker.

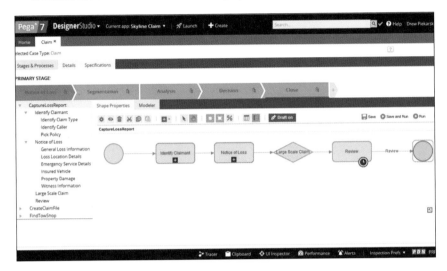

Processes pertaining to milestones or stages are easily designed by the business. Some of these processes or sub-cases will be executed sequentially. Others will be done in parallel. The stage definitions and transitions are simple and intuitive, yet powerful and complete. For instance, for each stage you can define the conditions, validation, and the policies to transition from one stage to the next. Examples of validation requirements include specific documents that need to be attached to the case, specific approvals, completion of specific processes, or just about any condition that makes sense to the business. The details of the process

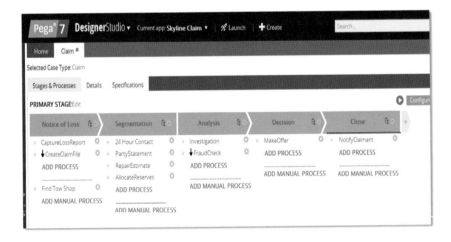

and the organization of processes in the case hierarchy can be completed by business analysts and process architects. Pega provides an outline of the processes involved in a case stage, ready for the next level of details of the process flow. The business analyst can design additional details of the process using either the shapes provided by Pega iBPM, or customized "smart" shapes to provide various reusable utilities to the process modeler.

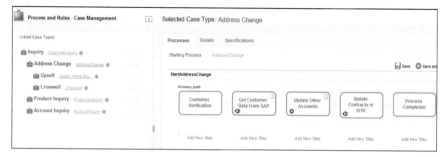

- **Hierarchical Case Design:** Dynamic cases are hierarchical. A parent case can have child sub-cases. There will be processes in each subcase that will generate tasks assigned to case workers. The details of the case types are captured and designed directly through Pega's DCO capabilities. The case type designer supports modeling the case hierarchy, the processes of each case type, and their dependencies. The designer also allow the definition of the roles and parties who will be performing the work, as well as the policies and procedures for each step, any external data sources or services that will be used in the case, and all the requirements for the case type.

- **The Case Portal:** For handling actual cases, Pega automatically creates a case portal where case workers and managers can view and analyze dynamic, real-time and actionable reports on case timeliness, completion throughput and the performance of various case workers. The same stage metaphor used in designing case types is presented to case workers and managers to show them how their work fits into the context of the overall case. The user has a 360-degree view of each case with several levels of detail, allowing users to view specific milestones or stages they have achieved and tasks that are still to be completed. The case portal is social-enabled through PegaPulse so that case workers can collaborate to resolve potential issues with specific cases.

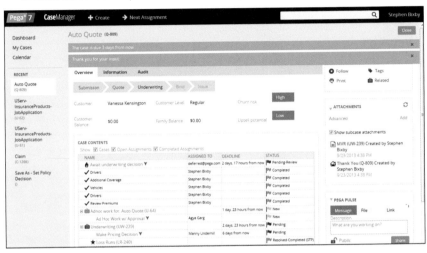

- Social Enablement: Through the Pega social networking capability PegaPulse, various roles in Pega iBPM solutions can collaborate via discussions, sharing documents, and even creating ad-hoc tasks or instantiating cases dynamically through the collaboration portal. The social networking capabilities are available in all phases of Pega iBPM solutions during both design and execution.

- **Mobile Enablement:** Pega provides extensive mobile iBPM capabilities to support mobile workers who can monitor and resolve cases. Pega applications are standards-based (HTML 5 + CSS 3 + JS) and provide design-once, run-anywhere capabilities to handle different operating systems, browsers, screen sizes and devices. Pega Mobile provides rich and comprehensive capabilities including support for signatures, audio attachments, QR and barcode scanning, as well as integration with third-party tools. Pega supports responsive web design (RWD) for mobile devices (as discussed in Chapter 6) to provide all of the Pega iBPM capabilities including tasks, cases, reports and charts. Pega Mobile also supports native mobile capabilities, such as the camera to snap and include pictures in dynamic cases or GPS to provide geo-based work assignment.

- **Ad-hoc Tasks and Dynamic Process Discovery:** In addition to planned processes, Pega supports unplanned, dynamic and ad-hoc tasks and processes. Through Pega's "design by doing" capabilities, a case manager can design a case type from an existing case instance and save it as a new case type so that changes to best practices are captured immediately for reuse.
- **Guided Interactions and Next-Best-Action:** Through Pega, policies and procedures become automated processes that guide the interaction of the worker. On browsers or mobile devices, the intelligence of real-time decisioning, situational business rules, as well as predictive and adaptive models assist the case worker with intuitive and targeted interactions. Contrast this to the typical business application that requires intense training and often cryptic or complex forms, multiple screens, manual perusing, and other wasteful activities that workers need to engage in to get their job done.

- Data and Documents from Multiple Internal and External Systems: Pega supports the CMIS standard discussed in Chapter 12. Pega is also a service producer and consumer with a very rich collection of connectors and services, including the Pega Process Extenders for SAP and Salesforce.com.

Sales
(Quotes, Purchase, Orders, etc.)

Customer Service
(Inquiries, Service Requests, Leads, etc.)

Example:
While viewing a Lead, create a Quote

Customer Onboarding

- **Federated Case Management:** In addition to its extensive Process Extender and service integration capabilities, Pega has pioneered federation of distributed cases, including the ability to create and view remote cases. These cases are accessed and used seamlessly via a unified case desktop and a central federated case repository.
- **Monitoring and Continuously Improving Dynamic Case Solutions:** As automated cases execute, the business stakeholders can monitor and introduce change dynamically. As work progresses and cases are processed, the stakeholders can make changes that keep processes under control in real time in order to meet business objectives. Pega iBPM provides dozens of out-of-the-box reports, and Pega's industry frameworks provide even more for specific industries and functions.

Prebuilt and custom-built reports can be organized, browsed, searched, and run from the report browser which provides intelligent drill down, aggregation, and pivot table behavior. In addition, the business-friendly browser lets designers create complex reports in seconds, selecting data from work tables and external systems. Users can easily customize, save, and share reports with title, column, filter, and sorting changes.

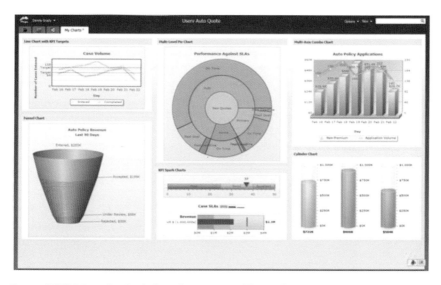

Pega iBPM for Optimizing Customer Experiences in Adaptive Enterprises

Pega iBPM's advanced analytics capabilities are designed to take the guesswork out of customer relationships. It accurately determines which people are going to be your best customers, what they are likely to want, how they will react to a particular offer, and how you can best align customer desires with business objectives.

Pega provides a complete suite of iBPM-enabled CRM capabilities including Pega Next-Best-Action Marketing, Pega Sales Force Automation, and Pega for Customer Service. Each of these CRM components offers all of the Pega iBPM features we have described here, such as automation of processes, dynamic cases, rich collection of rule types, analytics for decisioning, and support for both social and mobile.

For example, Pega for Customer Service provides an intuitive contact center desktop that guides service representatives through every step of a customer's case. In these interactions, Pega retrieves the situational scripting to make sure the right policies and procedures are consistently communicated to the customer. Decisioning models using predictive and adaptive analytics are leveraged in real time to anticipate the customer's needs, recommend the Next-Best-Action, and even suggest a relevant and timely offer, when appropriate. The Pega service solution provides unified channel management, including telephony integration, e-mail, chat, Web self-service, mobile, and social media monitoring and response that allows customers to start in any channel and seamlessly transition to another without losing context. Furthermore, Pega allows business users to simulate and test the potential impact of complex customer strategies before putting them into production. Once deployed, performance can be monitored and controlled at any level of operation, in real time.

Pega Next-Best-Action Marketing is an important milestone in the evolution of marketing automation software. The solution addresses marketing execution gaps by enabling organizations to focus on the customer and the customer lifetime value versus product-centric marketing. Real-time decisioning leverages predictive and adaptive analytics to balance the individual customer's needs with business objectives and determine the Next-Best-Action. As decisions can be executed over multiple channels, marketing becomes much more consistent across channels.

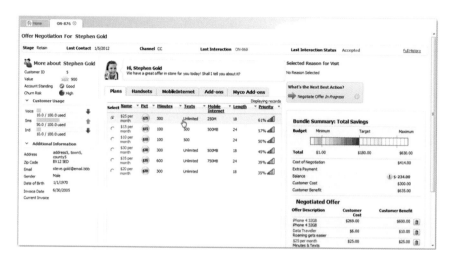

Pega Next-Best-Action Marketing reverses the traditional product/company-centric approach that pushes a product or service—often in bulk—to all existing and potential customers, regardless of the relevance of the offer. Pega attempts to optimize the value of each offer for each customer by personalizing the recommendations. Pega Next-Best-Action Marketing leverages predictive and adaptive models to add intelligence and relevance to offers by determining which customers are very likely to be interested. Thus, marketing actions depend on multiple very specific factors, such as the products owned by the customer, demographics, the history of the customer with the business, their potential lifetime value, and response to previous offers. This one-to-one approach to marketing enables organizations to optimize the customer experience. For instance, the focus for new customers can be on promoting products or services that help customers discover value from the company. For existing customers, specific and personalized up-sells and cross-sells can be offered that take into consideration what is known about the individual, such as age or location, and the history of the individual's relationship with the business.

Pega Next-Best-Action Marketing also supports real-time analytics and adaptive decisioning. Traditional marketing is often reactive, and it can takes weeks or even months to assess the impact of a marketing campaign. Pega leverages business-friendly analytical tools to explore the effectiveness of campaigns and offers immediately. This visibility into effectiveness across channels, customer segments and products could influence, for instance, which products should be marketed more than others, and in which regions. Furthermore, through adaptive analytics, the marketing solution continuously learns and adapts the campaigns or Next-Best-Action offers. It "listens" to customer decisions on offers, examines the outcomes, and adapts. The feedback from this automatic and adaptive learning can immediately influence the decisions on a campaign or offer for specific customers or segments of customers.

Why Pega iBPM: The 1080 High-Definition (HD) Panorama

In his seminal book *Customerpocalypse*,[47] Alan Trefler, the founder and CEO of Pegasystems Inc., provides a vision of the next-generation customers who are increasingly demanding to be in control. This is the era of a new generation of consumers: Generation D (Gen D) as Trefler defines it. Ignoring Gen D customers can put organizations at peril, as these are consumers who leverage social media and other channels to voice their opinions on the products and actions of a business with the goal of influencing the behavior of others. Gen D is determined to take viral reaction to the extreme.

Marketing to, selling to, and servicing this emerging generation of consumers requires a 1080 high-definition (HD) panorama of the customer. What is a 1080 HD panorama? Briefly, it puts each customer in high definition using three perspectives:

- **360° Data View:** This creates a holistic understanding of the customer from a data perspective. It puts the customer in the center and gathers all the data about that individual to provide the *what* about the customer.
- **360° Intent View:** The next perspective addresses the *what* and the *why*— the personality of the customer. Why does the customer come to you and what do you want to achieve with this customer? The what and why represent the *intent* of the customer.

---

[47] Trefler, Alan (2013). *Customerpocalypse.* Cambridge, MA: Pegasystems Inc.

- **360° Process View:** The last perspective is the *customer process view.* This perspective addresses the *when,* the *where* and the *how,* and is the most important *action* part of the 1080 HD customer panorama.

In order to achieve a 1080 HD panoramic view, you need a complete, holistic iBPM platform with all the capabilities described in this book. Pega is that platform. We began this book talking about the various business improvement methodologies, as well as process automation technologies, that are culminating in the adaptive enterprise. As we have seen, the accelerating pace of change means that the traditional methods for building solutions, such as custom, in-house coding and pre-built, packaged solutions, cannot keep up. The demand for change requires new ways of building business solutions as it is clear traditional approaches with stacks or packaged applications kill agility and thwart the adaptive, customer-centric enterprise.

Adaptive enterprises are responsive to change. The 1080 HD panorama enables them to manage change and address the requirements of Generation D consumers. Through Pega iBPM, enterprises are able to innovate and continuously improve without disruption—it's like being able to change the oil that runs the business while the engine is still running. This is quite a tall order, but through Pega iBPM, many Fortune 500 companies are making it a reality. Pega iBPM enables adaptive enterprises to leverage the amazing power that predictive analytics brings to business processes. It also exploits adaptive models to continuously learn and optimize, helping organizations discover models that can be enacted and deployed as robust business process solutions that can continuously improve. Perhaps the most important characteristic of an adaptive enterprise is to "Think big, but start small." Pega's approach is to start with small projects that can quickly generate value, succeed with them, radiate to additional sliver projects, and eventually transform the entire business into an adaptive enterprise.

Pega enables the adaptive enterprise to focus its efforts on building customer-centric solutions. One of the key ways Pega supports customer centricity is by providing the 1080 HD view of your customer. Pega is the only intelligent BPM platform that combines the 360° view of customer data with a 360° view of the business rules and decisions that represent the intent of the customer and the business, and a 360° holistic view of dynamic cases executed from end-to-end through the process. With this holistic 1080 HD panorama, details about the individual customer become clearer and intent is better understood. This clarity then enables the business to optimize the customer experience.

Most importantly, change becomes manageable by:

- **Empowering business units,** where business people can directly capture their objectives, design, change, and execute efficient processes, benefiting the customer.

- Fostering innovation, where organizations can launch new products and services quickly, and expand solutions globally by reusing and specializing business process assets in order to treat different customers differently.
- Enabling end-to-end dynamic case automation to handle collaboration and ad-hoc changes while eliminating costly, unnecessary work.
- Promoting business transformation by wrapping and renewing existing legacy systems.
- Delivering great customer experiences by leveraging predictive and adaptive analytics.

Pega iBPM helps adaptive enterprises optimize the customer experience and automate operations. Its Build for Change© technology empowers business people to create and evolve their critical business systems.

Pega iBPM is for customer-centric business applications.

It is the Next Wave for transforming adaptive enterprises. The journey begins...

REFERENCES

Benedict, T, et al. (2013). *BPM CBOK Version 3.0: Guide to the Business Process Management Common Body of Knowledge.* Retrieved from http://www.abpmp. org/?page=guide_BPM_CBOK

Christensen, C., & Raynor,M. (2003). *The Innovator's Solution: Creating and Sustaining Successful Growth.* Watertown, Massachusetts: Harvard Business Review Press.

Cisco (2013). "Internet of Everything." Accessed August 6, 2013. http://www.cisco. com/web/about/ac79/innov/IoE.html

Davenport, Thomas (2005). *Thinking for a Living.* Boston, Massachusetts: Harvard Business School Press.

Evans, Dave (2011). "Ten in Ten: Ten Technology Trends that will change the World in Ten Years." Paper presented at the Cisco Expo, Kiev, Ukraine, November 1-3, 2011.

Evans, Dave (2011). "The Internet of Things." Retrieved from http://www.cisco.com/ web/about/ac79/docs/innov/IoT_IBSG_0411FINAL.pdf

European Commission (2013). "Data Protection." Accessed August 6, 2013. http:// ec.europa.eu/justice/data-protection/index_en.htm

Fingar, Peter (2012). "Agent-Oriented BPM (aoBPM)—and a Confession." *BPTrends.* Retrieved from http://bptrends.com/publicationfiles/12-04-2012-COL-ExtComp-AgentOrientedBPM-Fingar%20%28SHLSeR5LQnSrTYYzb3R78w%29.pdf

Fowler, Martin (2003). *Patterns of Enterprise Application Architecture.* Boston, Massachusetts: Addison Wesley.

George, Michael (2003). *Lean Six Sigma for Service.* New York City, New York: McGraw-Hill.

Godratt, Eliyahu (2012). *The Goal: A Process of Ongoing Improvement, Third Edition.* Great Barrington, Massachusetts: North River Press.

Hammer, Michael (2001). *The Agenda: What Ever Business Must Do to Dominate the Decade.* New York: Crown Business.

IIBA and Kevin Brennan (2009). "A Guide to the Business Analysis Body of Knowledge (BABOK Guide)." Retrieved from http://www.iiba.org/BABOK-Guide.aspx

Kaplan, R.S., & Norton, D. P. (2004). *Strategy Maps: Converting Intangible Assets into Tangible Outcomes*. Watertown, Massachusetts: Harvard Business Review Press.

Kappelman, Leon (2010). *The SIM Guide to Enterprise Architecture: Creating the Information Age Enterprise*. New York City, New York: CRC Press, Taylor and Francis Group.

Khoshafian, Setrag (2011). *BPM: The Next Wave for Business Applications*. Cambridge, Massachusetts: Pegasystems Inc.

Khoshafian, Setrag (2006). "Business Process Management for Six Sigma Projects." In *2006 Workflow Handbook*, edited by Layna Fischer. Cohasset, Massachusetts: Workflow Management Coalition (WfMC).

Khoshafian, Setrag (2006). "Real-Time Six Sigma with BPM Suites." *BPTrends*. Retrieved from: http://www.bptrends.com/deliver_file.cfm?fileType=publication& fileName=10%2D06%2DART%2DReal%2DTimeSixSigma%2DKhosafian1%2Epdf

Khoshafian, Setrag (2009)."Managing Change with Re-Usable Assets for Government Agencies." In *2009 BPM and Workflow Handbook*, edited by Layna Fischer. Cohasset, Massachusetts: Workflow Management Coalition (WfMC). http://www. futstrat.com/books/handbook09.php

Khoshafian, Setrag (2008). "MyBPM: Social Networking for Business Process Management." In *2008 BPM and Workflow Handbook*, edited by Layna Fischer. Lighthouse Point, Florida: Future Strategies, Inc.

Khoshafian, Setrag (2010). "Predictive BPM." In *2010 BPM and Workflow Handbook*, edited by Layna Fischer, 61-71. Cohasset, Massachusetts: Workflow Management Coalition (WfMC). http://store.futstrat.com/servlet/Detail?no=79

Khoshafian, Setrag (2006). *Service-Oriented Enterprises*. Boston, MA: Auerbach Publications.

Khoshafian, S., & Schuerman,D. (2013). "Process of Everything." In *iBPMS: Intelligent BPM Systems*, edited by Layna Fischer. Lighthouse Point, Florida: Future Strategies, Inc., Book Division.

Khoshafian, S., Tripp, P., & Kraus, S. (2011). "Voice of the Network through Social BPM." In *Social BPM: Work, Planning and Collaboration under the Impact of Social Technology, 2011 BPM and Workflow Handbook*, edited by Layna Fischer. Lighthouse Point, Florida: Future Strategies, Inc., Book Division.

Khoshafian, S., & Walker, R. (2012). "Adaptive BPM." Retrieved from http://www.pega.com/sites/default/files/Adaptive-BPM-for-Adaptive-Enterprises-WP-May2012%20FINAL.pdf

Koulopoulos, T., & Champy, J. (2012). *Cloud Surfing: A New Way to Think About Risk, Innovation, Scale and Success (Social Century)*. Boston, Massachusetts: Bibliomotion.

Mahowald, R, & Sullivan, C. (2012). "Worldwide SaaS and Cloud Software 2012-2016 Forecast and 2011 Vendor Shares," *International Data Corporation*. http://www.idc.com/getdoc.jsp?containerId=236184

Oasis Content Management Interoperability Services (2012). "Oasis Standards." Last Modified June 21, 2012. https://www.oasis-open.org/standards

Odell, James. (2010). "Agent Technology: An Overview." Retrieved from http://www.jamesodell.com/Agent_Technology-An_Overview.pdf

O'Reilly Media Inc. (2012). *Big Data Now: 2012 edition*. Sebastopol, CA: O'Reilly Media.

The Open Group (2011). *TOGAF® Version 9.1*. Zaltbommel, Netherlands: Van Haren Publishing.

Reichheld, F., & Markey, R. (2011). *The Ultimate Question 2.0: How Net Promoter Companies Thrive in a Customer-driven World*. Watertown, Massachusetts: Harvard Business Review Press.

Schmidt, E. & Cohen, J. (2013). *The New Digital Age: Reshaping the Future of People, Nations and Business*. New York City, New York: Knopf Publishers.

Trefler, Alan (2013). *Customerpocalypse*. Cambridge, Massachusetts: Pegasystems Inc.

United States Congress House of Representatives (2011). *Federal Enterprise Architecture: A Blueprint for Improved Federal IT Investment Management and Cross-agency Collaboration and Information Sharing*. Washington D.C.: BiblioGov.

United States Department of Health & Human Services (2013). "Health Information Privacy." Last Modified August 6, 2013. http://www.hhs.gov/ocr/privacy/hipaa/understanding/srsummary.html

Wikipedia (2013). "Big Data." Last Modified July 29, 2013. http://en.wikipedia.org/wiki/Big_data

Wikipedia (2013). "Responsive Web Design." Last Modified July 26, 2013. http://en.wikipedia.org/wiki/Responsive_web_design

Wikipedia (2013). "Six Sigma." Last Modified August 28, 2013. http://en.wikipedia.org/wiki/Six_Sigma

Wikipedia (2013). "Shadow IT." Last Modified July 5, 2013. http://en.wikipedia.org/wiki/Shadow_IT

Wikipedia (2013). "Zettabyte." Last Modified July 29, 2013. http://en.wikipedia.org/wiki/Zettabyte

Williams, B., Gygi, C., Covey, S., & DeCarlo, N. (2012, Oct 16). *Six Sigma for Dummies.* Hoboken, New Jersey: For Dummies Publishing

Zachman International Enterprise Architecture (2012). "About the Zachman Framework." Accessed in 2012. http://www.zachman.com/about-the-zachman-framework

Zachman, John (2010). "Architecture is Architecture is Architecture." In *The SIM Guide to Enterprise Architecture: Creating the Information Age Enterprise,* edited by Leon Kappelman. New York: CRC Press, Taylor and Francis Group.

INDEX